Essays on Nonduality

Volume I

By

Todd Lorentz

Vedanta Publishing
Edmonton, Canada

Essays on Nonduality, Volume I
Copyright © 2017
By Todd Lorentz

All rights reserved. Printed in the United States of America. No part of this book may be used or reproduced in any manner whatsoever without written permission except in the case of brief quotations embodied in critical articles and reviews.

All rights reserved

ISBN: 978-0-9877782-1-5

First Edition, June 2017

Publisher contact:
Om@VedantaPublishing.com

Published by Vedanta Publishing
Edmonton, Canada
www.VedantaPublishing.com

This book is dedicated to
Maitreya, the World Teacher

Table of Contents

Introduction 1

Aesthetics and Nonduality............................ 10

From External Relations to Monism............... 24

Nonduality and the Sufi Tradition 60

A Challenge to Critical Theory
And Cultural Studies from Nonduality........... 76

Nonduality and Enlightenment
in Tibetan Buddhist Shamanism................. 116

Ramana Maharshi:
The Light of Advaita Vedanta....................... 143

Questioning Coercive State
Institutions from a Confucian Perspective.... 155

Nondualism and Bridging the
Gaps in International Development 169

Bibliography.. 193

The creation of this two volume set has been a meaningful experience and a labour of love. Projects of this magnitude often require the support and assistance of colleagues, friends and companions who donate their time and energy to assist in seeing it through to the end. My appreciation goes out to the visionary owners of the Juniper Bistro in Edmonton, Alberta and for the incredible atmosphere they and their staff create in support of artists, healers and families in the community. I would also like to thank Meryl for her computer skills and her patience with my endless revisions. My sincerest gratitude goes to two close colleagues for their deep and enduring friendship, their insights, humour and understanding. Most especially, I would like to thank Heather for her kindness and humility, her endless assistance with transcription and proofreading, and her dedication to a life of service and love.

Todd Lorentz
Edmonton, June 2017

Cover: the symbol of the perfect circle enclosing two vertical bars represents the world of duality contained within an all-embracing nondual reality.

Where there is separateness, one sees another, smells another, tastes another, speaks to another, hears another, touches another, thinks of another, knows another.

But where there is unity, one without a second, that is the world of Brahman.

This is the supreme goal of life, the Supreme treasure, the supreme joy. Those who do not seek this Supreme goal live on but a fraction of this joy.

—*Brihadaranyaka Upanishad*

Introduction

> All differences in this world are of degree,
> and not of kind, because oneness
> is the secret of everything.
> —*Swami Vivekananda*

It is hard to imagine that, of the many topics one could choose to write about, I have been drawn repeatedly to the subject of nonduality. This idea – that "everything is one" – has been at the centre of my thoughts since as far back as I can remember and it has caused me no shortage of internal struggle and conflict to make sense of a world which has made every effort to present itself to me as exclusively dualistic, material and fragmented. My immediate subjective experience is that I am functioning through a distinct and unique material body separate from, but relating to and interacting with, other subjects and objects in the material world. That is the picture which forms in my mind about the world, and these sensory impressions play a significant part in helping me to form my personal identity – my way of describing myself to other beings in the world. It seems like a pretty open-and-shut case and there is really nothing from this material existence to cause me to question this experience.

Yet my intuition – my *heart* – tells me that the fundamental nature of that same world is not as disconnected as I might first imagine. It tells me that I belong within something much more integrated and I, like many others around me, can occasionally witness moments of that wholeness. It is strange how one moment you can peer out at a landscape of trees, fields and mountains – a cacophony of contrasting shapes and colours – and then suddenly, as your mind settles into a sort of momentary stillness, you see the *Oneness* of it all. I am not talking about simply grasping the whole scene before you as one visual panorama. I mean that you experience in your mind a "knowingness" of the wholeness of life and your existence within that – not as some intellectual fact that can be dissected or analysed, but it comes upon your mind as a *presence* and *fullness of being*. Words cannot capture the entirety of the experience. It is as if you had touched the energies of life itself and it leaves you forever transformed. It is breathtaking...and sacred.

I see the effects of this same intuition in others around me. Some embrace it completely and go full "oneness", building into their daily lives the values and behaviours which arise from accepting that we are all interconnected and interdependent beings. Their lives demonstrate attempts to become less violent, more cooperative, less harmful in speech and action, and to become significantly more aware of everything around them. An increasing reverence for life becomes the hallmark of their *modus operandi* – even, at times, to their own detriment or disadvantage. An over-emphasis in this direction can lead to impracticality and a lack of common sense in dealing with the material world, the development of religious fundamentalism and spiritual isolationism.

Others, who may not experience the world or intuit life beyond the scope of mere subject-object relations, might occupy the opposite end of that pole – placing sensory experience and the observed facts of the material world as the foundations for truth and the limits of reality. Their lives demonstrate a type of mastery over the material world with a knack for scientific and material invention, a command over the resources of world around them and a capacity to manipulate ideas and beliefs in order to provide the substance for purpose and meaning in their lives. That is, as their focus and activity in the material world evolves, values and beliefs surrounding the accumulation of those material resources can change in order to provide justification and meaningfulness to their ventures. An over-emphasis in this direction can lead to materialism, egoism, scientism and disregard for the life within the form.

Most individuals, I am happy to say, find themselves in possession of a measure of both perspectives. They are able to appreciate the material limitations of the world in which they find themselves constrained along with the various capabilities needed to operate sufficiently in that material world. At the same time, they find the capacity to remain adequately receptive to an inner sense of the mystical, enough to warrant holding belief in an immaterial unseen universal power. This is no small trick – a walking contradiction of sorts – and without a suitably synthetic description of reality that can accommodate the fullness of both viewpoints, human beings have had to cobble together approaches to life which often result in constraints to the fuller or more purposeful expression of either. For the materialist – those whose focus is primarily concerned with the form side of life – success is measured by how much additional material benefit can be derived or secured in order to make their physical experience more pleasant and safe, although this pursuit can often create pressure to compromise spiritual meaning, purpose or moral justification. For the mystical or spiritual-minded individual, success is measured by increased sensitivity to moral principles and higher perceptions but whose life usually suffers from the possession of inadequate forms in the material world through which to express those ideals completely. In other instances, materialists can shrewdly adopt moralist positions in order to justify the proliferation of their material achievements, while the spiritual-minded can appropriate material resources to bear witness to the superiority of their moral positions.

Unfortunately, all of these viewpoints must also contain the germ of some measure of psychopathy, neurosis and psychosis wherever the resulting outlook is not entirely sincere or complete for the individual. Lacking a larger landscape which could not only accommodate but embrace the outer fragmented material life alongside the inner holistic spiritual and intuitive life, human beings are left forsaken on the battlefield of truth – sandwiched between the seemingly endless discrepancies between the life of spirit and of matter. Nonduality is such a synthetic worldview and its explanatory breadth has the power to both incorporate as well as transcend the presumed incongruity of those prevailing polarities.

From a bird's eye view, and in its simplest form, nonduality is easy to grasp. It simply requires the supposition that all of reality is one interconnected and interdependent existence –

Introduction

everything is One. This is really no different than holding the more familiar assumption – and, as the reader will come to see, it *is* an assumption – that the world is made up of disconnected and unrelated material objects and entities. You only need to be convinced of the possibility of its existence for the mind to begin searching for its trace in everyday life. The "One" has been variously described through the ages as the Whole, the Absolute, God, Brahman, the Quantum Field, the Cosmic Egg, Unbounded Consciousness and more. Liberation and enlightenment are terms that refer to a state of awareness where conscious-ness has literally 'liberated' itself from the confines of a finite material persona or personality to know its true identity as merely an aspect of the One.

A common analogy is used to illustrate this idea. Think about the multitude of waves dancing upon the surface of the ocean. Each one is unique and has a life and motion distinct for itself based on the prevailing conditions. Yet the wave is never separate from the ocean. It appears and disappears, rises and falls, and while it creates patterns and forms by which it can be recognised and identified it always remains a part of the ocean and subject to its life as a whole. The 'objects' and 'entities' of the world we live in are much like those waves upon the ocean – outer expressions in form of a deeper underlying whole. Our problem is that we are not dealing with simple material waves but with consciousness, and that individualised consciousness has mistakenly identified itself with the 'wave' instead of the 'ocean'.

In its technical aspects, nonduality can sometimes be a more difficult idea to grasp since

Introduction

the whole of it contradicts the way that we typically perceive and interpret the world. Even in the face of irrefutable logic and rationality, understanding that the world is a single, interconnected Whole is usually not a sufficient antidote to overcoming our moment to moment *experience* of a world as a separate or isolate being. It can be like stepping out over a chasm on top of a glass platform. Despite knowing that the glass is there and will support you it is hard to ignore the message that your senses are sending that you might be defying some natural law or principle of reality. Even more difficult is the challenge of de-conditioning (or re-conditioning) the mind from a pluralistic view of the world when the language we use is grounded in a belief of separateness. Language, in fact, is precisely the tool that we use to bridge the gap between two apparently distinct entities. Therefore, making postulations that our existence is based in nonduality simply appears erroneous and contradictory to our sensory experience of reality. One supposes that this is where faith could play a part.

Mystics, prophets and sages have pointed to the nondual essence of reality for millennia and, through a myriad of teachings and traditions, have shown us the Path, the Way, the Truth or the Tao. What seems to have escaped many western scholars and theologians these past centuries is that the canon of principles presented by the various spiritual teachers – including the Christ, Buddha, Confucius, Lao-Tzu, Krishna, Shankaracharya, Vyasa, Hermes and many more – were given *after* they had achieved some state of enlightened or liberated awareness. Their teachings followed upon the realisation they had achieved of the fundamental nondual unity and synthesis of reality. In seeing this, one could easily account for the various contradictions, gaps, distortions and paradoxes which have built their way into mainstream religious doctrine as a result of being presented from the perspective of duality and separateness – with each contradiction or paradox spawning the creation of more discord and division both within and between the various religious groups. In appreciating the nondual perspective from which the various spiritual teachers presented their principles, it would be justifiable to maintain that these teachers had intended to present the truth of nonduality openly and directly to the world – or to at least provide students with the techniques and tools through which they could eventually perceive that nondual reality. What is harder to defend is any claim that these same teachers of nonduality might present to their students a view about reality that was contrary to their experience or was an un-true or distorted account of what they had come to know as Truth. The principles of their various teachings, then, could never have rested on views based in a dualist or separative perspective, although I am certain they understood the challenge in presenting that to a following steeped in dualistic or material thinking. This should give one pause to reacquaint oneself with the various scriptures, sutras and tomes in the light of nonduality.

So a nondual frame of mind has to be 'earned'. It does not come about naturally in a mind dominated by a sensory experience of the world. It requires work, and it has to be *thought* about. That work starts with a theoretical

Introduction

acceptance of nonduality followed by persistent study and a further re-imagining and visualisation of the world around us in order to counteract the conditioned mind. Eventually, study gives way to concrete understanding and awareness of what nonduality is and how we can come to recognise it and live by its principles. This collection of essays has been assembled exactly for that reason, so that one might have access to an assortment of topics viewed through the lens of nonduality. The hope is that it can add to that growing body of knowledge which will deepen the imprint of nondualism on our consciousness.

This first book, in the two volume set, delves into a variety of interesting topics, the first of which is an examination of the role of nonduality in forming a coherent theory of aesthetics. That will lay the groundwork for a further survey of the role of nondualism and its interplay within the western philosophical tradition. The subsequent two essays investigate nondual principles in Buddhism and expose the challenges that nonduality faces with language as well as the way in which nonduality can be used as a tool in understanding enlightenment. Those more difficult themes are followed by essays presenting a lighter assessment of nonduality as it emerges in the practice of Sufism or through the life of Ramana Maharshi. In the final chapters, the need for coercive institutions in society is scrutinised under the lens of Confucian nonduality while, in the last essay, I provide an exploration of the effects that nonduality can have in changing our understanding of international development and poverty relief.

Introduction

I have made the attempt to include a broader range of topics – easy and difficult, familiar and obscure – sympathetic to the fact that nonduality often requires a number of approaches before a fuller understanding of the concept can occur. It might help the reader to know that no full appreciation of nonduality can be claimed until enlightenment occurs – a state which cannot be comprehended or described by words. That makes the study of nonduality a lifetime passion filled with unending discovery and inspiration. Each successful step in learning is not measured by accumulated knowledge but by a growing identification within oneself of the wholeness and infinite expanse which is our very nature. While each article presents its own particular style and premise, it may be in that momentary glimpse of a nondual reality, prompted by a slight turn of phrase or random statement, which can make the entire study worthwhile. That glimpse is of the sacred, and who could ask for more.

Aesthetics and Nonduality[1]

> As flowing rivers disappear in the sea, losing their names and forms, so a wise man, freed from name and form, attains the purusha, who is greater than the great.
>
> —*Mundaka Upanishad*

Within the circles of debate surrounding theories of aesthetic appreciation, one is apt to consider a substantial, and sometimes confusing, array of notions regarding the aesthetic appreciation of nature. The difficulty, for the most part, lies in providing an appropriate model for the appreciation of nature which does not, at the same time, *limit* nature as an artefact of anthropocentric fancy; allowing for a legitimate defence against environmental abuse or degradation. That is, one wishes to provide a model that can not only account for the external sensual features of nature that are aesthetically pleasing to human beings, but that also provides an account for our association with nature, experienced as an integral spiritual aspect of ourselves – and that might also provide standards for our interaction with nature.

These seemingly distinct accounts appear to manifest as contradictory notions. On the one hand, an account of external sensual features in nature requires a subject-object conception of the world in terms of a 'pluralism' or 'material

---

[1] This article was first published in *Axis Mundi*, University of Alberta, January, 2004 and has been revised, updated and re-edited for this book.

dualism' – describing the primary relationship between appreciator and the object of appreciation (i.e., nature) as between subject and object.[2] On the other hand, an account of our direct experience as a part of nature, and the moment-to-moment synthetic experience, entails a 'nondualistic' world view where the notion of a distinct subject and object become unified in a subtle but sublime experience of oneness. Nondualism can be properly defined as meaning "not-two" or "not separate" and describes a world view where all existence, seen and unseen, can be reduced to one underlying *Being* or *Whole*. In this conception of the cosmos, the *appearance* of separateness is real to the senses but the *actual* underlying essence of *reality* is interconnectivity and Oneness.

Thus, a fuller account of aesthetic appreciation is required which can acknowledge both our *material separation from* – as well as our *spiritual union with* – nature. Additionally, we need a model that can provide for the distinction between moments of *aesthetic appreciation, judgment or criticism* of nature (subject-object relationships) and events of *aesthetic experience* (of oneness) with nature. Toward these ends, I

---

[2] The notion of "pluralism" employed here denotes a world view that limits one's perspective to that of subject-object. That is, one views the world from an ego-centric position of subject separated from sense-experienced objects. While this, admittedly, describes our general view of the world it presents many logical problems when accounting for our emotional, psychological and, most importantly, spiritual experience of the world. One issue is that external sensual inputs cannot account for all the variety of internal experiences seen to arise in consciousness.

hope to show that an aesthetic model can exist which fulfills all of these requirements. I will refer to this model as the *Nondual Model of Aesthetic Appreciation in Nature*.

The Nondual Model of Aesthetic Appreciation

Until now, aesthetic criticism in art has been limited to the purely pluralistic account of subject-object. This limit has caused some difficulties when transferring that account to our experience in nature. While we have become somewhat proficient at critically assessing the objective forms of nature, this approach often falls short in accounting for the deeper communion and unity we might experience in art, or in nature. Subsequently, arguments relying on determinations about the aesthetic value of *external* objects fail to substantiate a clear standard in issues of environmental restoration. The physical apparatus of the human being registers "objective' features in nature such as shape, colour, texture, smell, sound and taste. Many current models of *aesthetic appreciation*, which mainly approach this topic from a pluralistic standpoint, can account for these features; relating the attributes of forms to the sensory experiencer.

But what of the deeper sense of "oneness" which an appreciator may encounter in nature? The nondual model *can* provide a thorough account for this view. R. W. Hepburn alludes to this deeper sense and attempts to formulate the notion of an aesthetic experience in nature distinct from the simple subject-object relationship.

We have not only a mutual involvement of spectator and object, but also a reflexive effect by which the spectator experiences *himself* in an unusual and vivid way; and this difference is not merely noted, but dwelt upon aesthetically. The effect is not unknown to art, especially architectture. But it is both more intensely realized and pervasive in nature experience – for we are *in* nature and a part *of* nature; we do not stand over against it as over against a painting on a wall.[3]

Other models, like the metaphysical imagination model,[4] offer a deep immersion into the aesthetic experience of oneness but, failing in reverse, cannot account sufficiently for our pluralistic experiences of subject-object.

The *Nondual Model of Aesthetic Appreciation* admits of two aspects in aesthetics. First, nonduality does not exclude or deny the existence of pluralistic perspective of our sensory experience. It simply recognises it as one component of our total encounter with the world around us. For the Nondualist, a pluralistic account occurs as the experiencer perceives, from within themselves, a subjective standpoint in relation to an object; the attention of the appreciator fragmented as a subject separate from the object, taking cues about the perceived object through the senses. The appreciator can

---

[3] R. W. Hepburn. "Contemporary Aesthetics and the Neglect of Natural Beauty", *British Analytical Philosophy*. Editcd by Bernard Williams and Alan Montefore. (Routledge and Kegan Paul Ltd.: London, 1996), 289-290.
[4] Allan Carlson. *The Aesthetics of Nature: An Introduction*, pre-publication, 9-10.

then evaluate the objective form, based on those cues, in a state of *disinterestedness*.[5]

The *second* aspect within the nondual perspective requires a shift of attention that is much more difficult to achieve. The appreciator *detaches their attention* from their own egocentric grounding to reformulate their perceptual standpoint into a state of "pure experience". This requires a considerable mental discipline familiar to many meditative disciplines found throughout many mystical traditions. Meditative approaches involving "psychological de-centralisation" facilitate the shift from a pluralist perspective to a singular nondual one. The barriers of "mentally perceived separateness" are dissolved and the appreciator no longer "psychologically" exists. What remains is a pure experience of oneself and nature as One with the appreciator experiencing an essential oneness with nature. Like the carefree experience of nature one might have during childhood (a period of human development which significantly lacks ego structures), a psychologically experienced unification of subject and object can sometimes be invoked whereby one becomes "fused" experientially with the environment. There is no longer a psychological appreciator (subject) and appreciated nature (object) but simply one substantial experience of *Being*.

This model resembles, in many ways, the engagement model offered by Arnold Berliant[6]

---

[5] This is a common feature in many models of appreciation allowing the critic to eliminate some personal bias. I have no particular exception to the application of this standard mental perspective and so would accept the use of this procedure here as well.

wherein an emotional relationship arises between the appreciator and the environment. However, it provides a clearer demarcation and understanding between the appropriate use of *aesthetic experience* and *aesthetic criticism* or *judgment*. The nondual model does this by distinguishing between the essential features of the aesthetic experience and the accidental features required for aesthetic appreciation and criticism. It is important, then, to clarify these terms as employed through this approach. There exists, for the nondual perspective, two similar approaches to both art and nature[7] – as *aesthetic experiencer* and as *aesthetic appreciator*.

The *aesthetic experiencer* begins with the notion of detachment, but employs this toward his/her *own* personal identity or ego-centric perspective. In detaching from their own sense of identity as an observing subject the individual can begin to dissolve the perceived sense of separateness form the object. This is, admittedly, a difficult position to achieve and involves a practiced mental discipline to offset our mentally conditioned ego-centric perspective.[8] Primarily,

---

[6] Arnold Berliant. "The Aesthetics of Art and Nature." *Landscape, Natural Beauty and the Arts*. Edited by Salim Kemal and Ivan Gaskell. (New York: Cambridge University Press, 1993).

[7] As we will come to see, this model will work equally well for objects viewed as art or as nature in itself. In fact, this view may hold for any situation in the human experience.

[8] Actually, there can be said to be two ways to achieve this position. The first requires a practiced mental discipline, often involving many years to master, to facilitate the *intentional* release from the ego-centric perspective. The second method is more spontaneous,

the analytical discourse of the mind drops and the notion of a subject-object separation is transcended. The process involves an intentional shift of awareness out of oneself as an experiencing subject and into a state of directly experiencing without the interference or bias of a "psychological *experiencer*" imposing itself upon the moment. A pure and direct experience may result wherein the sole factor falling within the scope of awareness is the experience of "Being". The *experiencer* may then be described as *registering* the experience with little or no cognitive discrimination overriding that direct experience. If at any time the activity of cognitive assessment begins to reassert itself the individual necessarily defaults back into a condition of *appreciator*.

The *aesthetic appreciator* attitude is quite different from the mind-set of the *aesthetic experiencer*. In the former position, the individual retains the ego-centric perspective but includes the attitude of disinterestedness *towards the subject*. The subject-object relationship remains intact and the physical senses are employed to provide the content of sensory input from which to judge, appreciate or criticise the object of appreciation. This is a cognitive phase where one can reflect upon the impact that the features in the perceived form have on the aesthetic sensitivities of the subject or individual. As the

---

sometimes brought on in moments of mental fatigue or surrender, which *unintentionally* releases one from the ego-centric perspective. During periods of childhood, when the structures of the ego are not fully developed, this experience can be more common.

Aesthetics and Nonduality

aesthetic critic, evaluation or appreciation is then rendered about the object under scrutiny.

These two states of experience need not be totally exclusive of one another and may overlap in a variety of ways. For instance, we may dislike the visual features of a particular landscape in relation to our cognitive analysis of the object and, at the same time, experience a sense of communion with nature that cannot be accounted for simply through the observed features in that landscape. Likewise, we may repeatedly appreciate a particular landscape for its cognitive aesthetic qualities but experience an inner sense of imbalance or disconnection within it. The degree to which one can hold a state of detachment from egocentricity will determine the intensity of the aesthetic experience while an increase in one's cognitive activity will increasingly distance one from the sense of communion or synthesis with the nature of the landscape.

An example may serve to illustrate the point more thoroughly. Several years ago I was fortunate to be living near a lake in rural Alberta. During the winter months I would take the opportunity to enjoy the raw beauty of this idyllic setting and on a regular basis I would take nightly walks out into the center of the frozen lake. You could hear the whiplash sounds of large cracks forming in the ice as they whipped across the surface of the vast frozen expanse. The jet black sky above was awash with the sparkle of a billion stars and the air was crisp and dense, punctuated occasionally by sounds of a coyote or a car echoing from miles away through the dense cold air. On one such occasion my mind had fallen away from the considerations of daily life and my sense of position, in relation to the shoreline, had completely dissolved into an intense awareness of the sublime view above me. All thoughts and notions of my individual "self" slowly faded into obscurity. At once, an intense experience of oneness washed over my consciousness and obliterated the remaining fragments of separation. All sensations of time and space were lost and there was, for a moment, only one complete and whole instance of *Being*. This experience lasted only a short while and, as it came to my attention that "I" was, in fact, experiencing this moment the thoughts and perspectives of that "I" flooded back into my awareness and experience. After some minutes it had completely pushed the essence of that experience into the background. Afterwards, I marvelled at memories of that rapturous jewel-studded sky but was unable to re-capture that same particular experience of oneness with nature. For many months I pursued the same adventurous routine but could not achieve that state of mind wherein my thoughts ceased to interfere with the moment of experience. This held true in spite of the fact that on many occasions, *critically* speaking, even more aesthetically pleasing and elaborate night skies were encountered. The original experience clearly indicated to me that the *aesthetic experience* of nature was something quite apart from the *aesthetic judgment* or *appreciation* of the sensual features of nature. While I was able to more fully appreciate subsequent detailed examinations of nature's beauty, this was plainly quite distinct from the direct *aesthetic experience* of "oneness" with nature. It became apparent to me that there were distinct perceptions of "reality" possible which required a definite shift in awareness in order to apprehend and which bestowed upon me an innate intrinsic value for nature.

The *Nondual Model of Aesthetic Appreciation* can fully account for both the *aesthetic experience* of nature as well as the "formal" *aesthetic appreciation* of nature. Like its other applications in philosophy, nonduality does not exclude the pluralistic "subject-object" approach to events; it merely recognises the pluralistic perspective as functioning within a sub-category of experience – namely, form and physical sense perception. It also admits that this narrow band of experience appears as the most prominent to us, owing to the fact that the familiar impressions imposed upon us by our sensory apparatus condition our experience of the world.

The implications of the *Nondual Model of Aesthetic Appreciation* suggest, in relation to nature, at least two things. *First,* to some extent, nature can be treated like art. That is, focusing entirely within the limits of the pluralistic perspective, the *appreciation* of nature can utilise many cognitive or emotional considerations to provide a critical assessment, judgment or evaluation of the aesthetic qualities in nature. My intention has not been to provide those criteria here. The *natural environmental model*,[9] for instance, can provide a comprehensive cognitive account for the appreciation of nature

---

[9] Allen Carlson. "Appreciation and the Natural Environment," *The Journal of Aesthetics and Art Criticism.* XXXVII 3, Spring 1979.

by a subject who is objectifying nature in this way.[10]

Secondly, and more importantly for our purposes, the *aesthetic experience* can provide a deeper understanding of our innate connection to nature and, at the same time, advances a powerful argument against environmental abuse or mistreatment. Fundamentally speaking, the *aesthetic experience* of nature grounds our intuitions and identity *in* nature and, as such, substantiates an intrinsic value in nature and precludes its misuse from the outset. A monistic understanding of our actual conscious unity with nature demands that we consider our actions on nature prior to engaging in economic or social enterprises that may, in any way, affect the condition of nature. To harm or radically alter nature would be seen as harming or radically altering ourselves – regardless of our preconceived notions of what nature should supply us. This is not possible solely through mere individually subjective critiques of nature since such judgements can be as diverse as there are individual opinions. On the other hand, an

---

[10] While the *natural environmental model* can provide a thorough account for the essential criteria of *aesthetic appreciation* it, like many other models that assume the perspective of subject-object pluralism, must often hold the view that *aesthetic experience* (as an experience of oneness with nature) is, in some way, trivially [incidentally] related to *aesthetic appreciation*. As a result, its movement toward an ethic of restoration must be generated out of the criteria for *aesthetic appreciation*. Under a monistic framework, however, the *aesthetic experience*, itself, generates an intrinsic value to underlie an ethic of restoration.

aesthetic experience of nature is universal. Only in this way can a common spiritual appreciation be sufficient to provide common standards for our interactions with nature.

This removes us entirely from the problematical approach of justifying nature in terms of our *aesthetic appreciation* of it. It requires us to consider, *prior* to any notions of aesthetic value, whether an activity would be worthy in nature as if we were to perform it upon *ourselves*. For example, would we consider 'mining" a kidney from our own body simply for profit? Should we extract a renewable resource, such as blood, at a rate that is unsustainable? An ethic derived from *aesthetic experience* is more immediate to us than one from *aesthetic appreciation*, which is much more vulnerable to manipulation from individual ideologies or self-serving viewpoints, and it appeals to our sense of "oneness" with nature prior to disruptive environmental activities.

In the example above, we might deem "donating blood" an acceptable practice insofar as we moderated that harvest, did no harm to ourselves, and took measures to prevent a radical or negative alteration of our health. Likewise, in situations of environmental interference, a nondual synthetic appreciation of nature would encourage us to moderate the harvest of renewable resources, prevent harm to the system as a whole, and take measures to prevent a radical or negative alteration of a healthy ecosystem. This may entail a pronounced limit, or even radical departure, from currently exercised economic and social practices within nature. It may even require a dramatic departure from the present living standards encountered almost exclusively in the industrialized nations. However, the safeguarding of opulence, luxury and the pursuit of wealth is not a sufficient defence against the need to make changes to present attitudes in the treatment of nature. The desire for living standards over and above basic necessities could never, practically speaking, outweigh the health of the environmental system which supplied the materials for those standards.[11]

Our spiritual connection to the world, whether through objects of art or in nature itself, is often experienced but seldom encompassed entirely within an aesthetic model of appreciation.[12] The *Nondual Model of Aesthetic Appreciation* appeals to both *aesthetic apprecia-*

---

[11] While questions such as "what limits are there to basic necessities?" are important, they fall outside of the present attempt to describe the *Nondual Model of Aesthetic Appreciation* itself. It is admitted, though, that it will require further serious consideration. It is also recognised that the western industrial market economies will not easily accept what may amount to a lesser standard of *material living*, although that need not imply a lesser *quality of life* as a whole. Some would argue that the intense pluralistic focus on *material wealth* in market economy nations has served to undermine the *aesthetic experience* of communion with nature and, quite obviously, the *spiritual* foundations within western society.

[12] Many models tend to fall either on the side of sensual form appreciation or on an emotional engagement with nature. Few, however, are able to provide an underlying thesis to account for both approaches as completely as the nondual model can. In addition to this, the model provides an account for the *necessary* approach to nature when considering activities of interference.

tion and *aesthetic experience* by recognising two distinct perspectives in approaching the world and, as a result, provides a great deal of explanatory power. While we can choose to focus our attention solely within the pluralistic sensory experience of the subject-object we can also work to detach from our ego-centric viewpoint in order to experience our inner spiritual connection with nature itself. This latter view demands a consideration of our activities on nature as a part of *what* we are prior to the alteration of the outer forms and features of nature that, subsequently, become the subject of that *aesthetic appreciation.*

From External Relations to Monism

> Oneness is like the clear blue sky—everything arises, unfolds, and subsides within its all-compassionate love... Everything is an aspect of Oneness. And our quest to know this comes from Oneness.
> —*Abhinavagupta*

I have had an interest in the spiritual life for many years and first came to monism through encounters with eastern philosophy. I was surprised to learn that there were serious clusters of monism in the history of western philosophy.

I subsequently pursued an investigation of monism and nonduality for "intuitive" reasons, and thought that it was important to what kinds of impact monism can have on an ordinary person's life. Raised in a rural setting, I was often struck by the sense of sheer presence, rhythm and interconnectivity in nature. This feeling remains with me to this day.

It is difficult to account for this quality of deep inner synthesis as arising merely from the random material forces of mutation or blind evolution. That perspective has often felt both empty and alienating to me and served little more than to promote a sense of spiritual isolation. It is my feeling that this type of alienation, evidenced now on a global scale, has profoundly influenced our society and our environment in negative ways. Wherever we have viewed ourselves as individual units, set apart from nature, our sense of respect and responsibility toward each other has diminished.

A healthy and integrated community is fundamental to our own well-being and further alienation leads to the breakdown of societal values and even our deepest sense of 'self'. In distancing ourselves from nature, and from each other, we become psychologically and spiritually separated from the roots of our own *beingness* in the world.

When I first came to monism, I was impressed by the fact that monism did not discount my *sensual* experiences of the material world; it simply described that material world as a characteristic of the universe in which those experiences could occur. Yet it provided a viewpoint of unity and coherence which underwrote that material world, and which could explain the aspects of myself which were not material. *Monism* can be properly defined as "the theory that all things are derived from one single ultimate source."[1] To admit to an external dualistic perspective of the world does not entail the denial of an ultimate underlying nondual reality. Pluralism and materialism alone seemed insufficient to account for phenomena like intuition, mystical experiences and even the nature of consciousness itself. Deterministic theories founded upon materialistic concepts are logically complete *without* the need for consciousness and so they explain nothing at all.

---

[1] Peter A. Angeles. *Dictionary of Philosophy.* (Barnes and Noble Books: New York, 1981), 178. A further reading of the text provides the following perspective on monism: "1). The theory that all things in the universe can be reduced to (or explained in terms of) the activity of one fundamental constituent (God, matter, mind, energy, form), 2). The belief that reality is One, and everything else is illusion."

According to the best current theories in materialist science today, there exists *no role* in evolution for consciousness. In fact, there exists no purpose or place for consciousness *at all*. It is simply an accidental accoutrement with no apparent function other than to inadvertently and involuntarily witness what unfolds before it. And yet, consciousness is the very center of our day to day existence and often demonstrates the capacity to transcend the boundaries of mere physicality. It seems to me that consciousness, with all of its mysterious events, must occupy a more *essential* role in the world than what either Materialists or Reductionists seem able to offer. A nondual outlook can offer a perspective that not only includes consciousness as a significant characteristic of the universe but provides a place for consciousness as vital, necessary and intrinsic to the unfolding of universe.

I believe my own explorations into monism have provided a foundation from which to see myself integrally connected with the world around me. To view one's self as fundamentally united with nature engenders a respect for all relationships in life. Monism nurtures that responsibility toward the welfare of others and provides a framework to develop desired characteristics like cooperation, compassion and love. The implications of this are hopeful when seen against the backdrop of the current global divisions along cultural, religious, moral and economic lines. In a world rich with diverse and, sometimes, contrary beliefs one would hope to discover an enduring moral attitude in which to accommodate that diversity while fostering an underlying unity. Monism upholds such an attitude by endorsing the variety of personal and cultural manifestations as distinct and unique expressions of one whole. Moulded within the atmosphere of free market capitalism, many in the west have been enchanted by values that favour ruthless competition and an achievement of "success" measured only in terms of material acquisition and consumer power. Seeing the world through a monist perspective offers the opportunity to re-evaluate this mindset and modify our social priorities. Values rooted in merciless competition conflict with notions of wholeness and unity. Members of society, pitted against each other for basic needs, material commodities, or even self-esteem involve themselves in little more than systematic spiritual cannibalism. This constantly militates against any attempt to realise world unity. It makes little moral sense to empower some members of the whole at the expense of others. To persist in these endeavours can only serve to threaten social coherence, moral legitimacy and even human survival. A humanely sound monistic approach to life could provide a perspective in which to rehabilitate economic, political and educational priorities along lines conducive to the expression and development of compassionate social systems.

    Since my earliest recollections I have been fortunate to have had inner glimpses of the fundamental unity of our existence. This feeling has provided for me a sense of belonging – a benediction of sorts – and has generated a keen interest in understanding both my own nature and its place in the universe. I am not unique in seeking answers to these questions and share this journey with many. My own exploration led me to investigate a variety of philosophical and religious views and it was through eastern philosophy that I had my first encounters with complex ideas of monism and nonduality.

I was later surprised to discover, scattered throughout the assortment of western thinkers and ideas, a variety of viewpoints arguing either for or from a monistic position. My astonishment stemmed from what had appeared to me as the obvious indifference to monism that I had experienced in society from both scientific and religious influences. The impression arose that monism was far too subtle to justify, and perhaps even wholly ineffable. It seemed to me, however, that this view was mistaken. In fact, the history of western philosophy contains an abundant variety of interesting forms of monism portrayed by some of the most respected philosophers within the tradition. Thus, I hope to demonstrate to the reader that monism, within the western philosophical tradition, is both significant and effable, and deserves much more attention from philosophers and other academics in articulating this view to the public. Although far from comprehensive, this exploration may help to illustrate the solid grounds upon which monism resides and provide some idea of the evolution of western thinking which has occurred through the centuries.

The history of monism in western philosophy contains a rich variety of approaches from the earliest recordings of Greek thought up to and including some of the most recent theories in consciousness and quantum mechanics. With its often innate coherence and rigorous explanatory power, monism has spurned attempts, time and again, to be laid to rest by the march of philosophical inquiry. While monism, in general, describes a view of the universe as a unified synthetic Whole, the method of approach has embraced two distinctly different lines – namely, *qualitative* monism and *quantitative* monism. *Qualitative* monism asserts that the universe is made of one kind of substance or element – perhaps fire or water – from which all objects are constructed whereas, *quantitative* monism posits the existence of the universe as one Unified Whole or *Being*, of whose manifestations are simply objectified attributes or properties of that One.

The earliest proponents of *qualitative* monism emerged in Pre-Socratic philosophy. Thales of Miletos (625-546 BC), founder of the Milesian school, asserted that all features of the manifested universe, regardless of their objective properties, consisted of only one quality. Thales sought to understand the primary element providing the material cause for the known physical universe by moving beyond the acceptance of a mere cosmological myth. Given the variety of shapes and states that it could portray, the primary element and material cause was thought to be *water*. The particular "mixture" or "concentration" of such a quality accounted for a variety of forms and features found in nature. The philosophy of Thales can be classified correctly as a form of *hylozoism*[2] – the notion that all objects are invested with life. While few of his works survive to this day, much

---

[2] Ranade, R. D. and Kaul, R. N. "Pre-Socratics" *History of Philosophy Eastern and Western, Vol. II* Edited by Sarvepalli Radhakrishnan. (Unwin Brothers Limited: London, 1953), 29.

of what we know of him has been passed to us through the works of Aristotle.

On the basis of Aristotle's cautious remarks it can be inferred that Thales thought of the world as perfectly understandable through the idea of water – [the constituent] essential to life (and thus to self-motion), versatile, common, and powerful enough to every physical phenomenon.[3]

While very little else can be said of the ideas of Thales, we can see the first historical movements away from a reliance on myth towards a reasoned conception of the physical world as qualitatively monistic.

The notion of a Primary Substance, defined as one of the elements, was soon after to be questioned. Anaximander (610-546 BC), a devout pupil of Thales', wondered how one of the particular elements, such as water, could be the unique quality. For instance, it was inconceivable that any other qualities could even exist if the instantiation – water – were infinite. Instead, he posited the existence of a first principle called the Boundless or Unlimited (*Apeiron*), infinite and indestructible, from which physical elements found their source and eventual destination.

> This Apeiron surrounds and embraces all things and apparently 'steers' or governs them as well. It seems to have been conceived as ungenerated as well as imperishable, thus contrasts in every respect with the limited, perishable world it engenders...

---

[3] *The Encyclopedia of Philosophy, Vol. VIII* Edited by Paul Edwards. (MacMillan Publishing Co., Inc.: New York, 1967), 97.

> The Boundless transcends the processes of world creation, circumscribing each individual world in space, outlasting all of them in time, and providing the inexhaustible material source, the eternal motive power, the vital energy, and (presumably) the geometrical form and cyclical regularity for the cosmic process as a whole.[4]

While the notion of the *Apeiron* might be seen as an attribute, it was most assuredly regarded as a limitless substantive and material constituent in the creation of the physical world. This unlimited constituent provided grounds for a monistic perspective on the universe.

Another Pre-Socratic, Anaximenes, followed shortly after Anaximander and further developed the doctrines of Thales. He became the first to proclaim a true *Theory of Primary Substance*, although, differing from Thales, he advanced *air* as the ultimate basis of all material transformation. Through a process of condensation and rarefaction, the proximity and distance between particles of air altered to become fire, liquid and finally solid.

> The fundamental and most pervasive thing in the world is air (*aer*), according to Anaximenes. Air is infinitely vast in extent but perfectly determinate in character: It is ordinary atmospheric air, invisible where most even in consistency, visible through the and Cold and Damp and motion. It is from air that all things that exist, have existed, will exist, come into being. This applies to gods and divine things and also to the rest of the world, inasmuch as the world is compounded out of the offspring of air. On this account, Anaximenes suggests, the primordial air is

---

[4] *The Encyclopedia of Philosophy*, Vol. I, 118.

continually in motion, and this motion the cause of alternating physical states.[5]

Anaximenes seems to prefer a blend of monism and pluralism. All things, therefore, take their shape and consistency from this one Infinite pervasive substance. Difficulties arose in making his theory persuasive even though he was able to develop a coherent system of laws regarding the development of the physical world.

Herakleitos (535-475 BC), a bold and original thinker, considered a type of "living fire" to underlie the ever-living, but constantly changing, world. More importantly, he was one of the first to definitively claim that the many forms, experienced as independent and conflicting, were really one. His theory of the *Strife of Opposites* led to a view of the universe which was constantly 'attuning' itself from the One to the many, and from the many to the One. These opposites, bound so inseparably to one another, provided him with a notion of a monistic universe. "The unity of opposites struck Herakleitos so forcibly that he leaped to the conclusion that all things are one."[6] This talk of perpetual flux and exchange of "living fire", if taken in more symbolic terms, gave the clearer notion of the One as an energy or active force underlying the myriad forms in the material world. His philosophical conception suggested a view of existence possessing a vast will-to-become realised through the extensive and ongoing interplay of forces. The difficulty of understanding and interpreting the works of

---

[5] *The Encyclopedia of Philosophy*, Vol. I, 118.
[6] *The Encyclopedia of Philosophy*, Vol. III, 477.

Herakleitos often resulted in generally unfavourable opinions of his philosophy.

While many of these ideas, descriptive of formal qualitative monism, failed to endure the contemporary stream of investigation, they stand as a testament to the bold and courageous inquiry undertaken by these early sages and mystics. What followed was a spirited shift in philosophy towards quantitative monism; whereby the universe turns out to be viewed as One Being – a single Organism or Individual.

One of the earliest examples of *quantitative* monism in the West arose from the philosophy of Parmenides of Elea (c. 515 BC). As the founder of the Eleatic school, Parmenides offered a rigorous analytical approach to truth in which he put forth the conclusion that there is only *Being* – its qualities being timeless, ungenerated, everlasting and indestructible. His main works are divided into two poems, *The Way of Truth* and *The Way of Seeming*, depicting a revelation by the Goddess of "plain truth" in the former and the "deceptive beliefs of men" in the latter. This approach became known as *The Doctrine of Being*. Positing a standard principle from which one must follow, Parmenides argued that "only that can *Be* which can be thought: for thought exists for the sake of what is."[7] Accordingly, "non-Being" could not exist as it would present an impossible proposition. The process of analytical reasoning, stringently arranged throughout *The Way of Truth*, gives us, in this view, a necessary condition for the universe:

---

[7] Renade, 36.

...consider the consequences of saying that anything *is*. In the first place, it cannot have come into Being. If it had, it must have arisen from nothing or from something. It cannot have arisen from nothing; for there is no nothing. It cannot have arisen from something; for there is nothing else than what is. Nor can anything else besides itself come into Being; for there can be no empty space in which it could do so.... If it *is*, then it is now, all at once.[8]

In this way Parmenides showed that, given a really sound analysis of the notions, there could only be *Being* (One); complete, ungenerated, whole, ever-existing and infinite. Having put forward this account of 'truth', he described the illusions that mortal men experience having their roots in ignorance and lack of knowledge. *The Way of Seeming* points to the pluralistic experience of what there is. This illusion leads to discussions of becoming or of non-existence which, as was shown earlier, could not logically arise. Therefore, the supposed world of appearances seems to be pluralistic but must be, in the end, either a mere illusion or simple aspects of one grand spiritual *Being*. The work of Parmenides demonstrated a powerful affinity between analysis and monistic ideology. It also indicated that a sturdy foundation, through analytical philosophy, could be generated to substantiate the monistic intuitions of countless mystics.

One mystic, who stands alone in that early period of Greek thought and who deserves a special mention, was Pythagoras (c.582-506 BC). Fusing the elements of science and religion,

---

[8] Renade, 36.

Pythagoras emphasized a view that the universe had a discreet mathematical order which could provide foundations for a religious or sacred way of life. Above all, philosophy was to be lived; and a thorough scientific study of the mathematical principles in nature could provide the way. Proportion and harmony in numbers revealed for him an insight into proportion and harmony in nature, including the human experience. Like one who draws definitive conclusions in mathematical deduction, Pythagoras became convinced that everything in the manifested universe begins with and reduces to *One*. In natural terms, thought, too, was *One*; everything else dealt with the "other" and so followed numerically and pluralistically from that *One*. As a blueprint for existence, concepts from both mathematics and religion could be seen to mutually reflect a deeper order in the universe that could be both known and lived. Pythagoras showed that mathematics provided an exact tool with which to describe the opus of the Cosmos. His notion continued to create breakthroughs in our ways of knowing the world to this day.

Making use of the Eleatic view of absolute monism Zeno of Elea (c. 489 BC), a student of Parmenides', put forward a series of negative arguments against the dogmatic defenders of pluralism. Instead of arguing directly in support of monism he simply adopted the truth of the pluralist's position and then proceeded to deduce from it an array of contradictory conclusions and logical absurdities (*reductio ad absurdum*). His arguments became known as *Zeno's Paradoxes* and are still recognized as "immeasurably subtle and profound".⁹ To illustrate the approach used by Zeno, we might look at his second argument against plurality:

> (P1) If there are many, it is necessary that they be as many as they are, neither more nor fewer. But if they are as many as they are, they must be *finite*.

> (P2) If there are many, the existents must be infinite. For there are always other [existents] between existents, and again others between these.¹⁰

Thus the existents are *infinite*.

> (Conclusion) If there are many, then they are both *finite* in quantity and *infinite* in quantity. This conclusion provides a paradox, therefore, there can only be One and pluralism must be false. ¹¹

While some have worked to refute his arguments against pluralism, the limitations of the pluralist's conceptions remained poignantly transparent. Zeno often used short stories and parables to illustrate how the notion of a universe, comprised of separate and autonomous "entities", can often lead to contradictions in dialectical argument.

Parmenides had also claimed that motion was an illusory attribute and Zeno additionally provided a number of arguments illustrating the contradictions in the dualistic notion of movement between two locations. One well known

---

⁹ Renade, 38.
¹⁰ This premise assumes that there can be no *empty space* or "*nothingness*" between physical objects.
¹¹ *The Encyclopedia of Philosophy, Vol. VIII*, 371.

account is the argument of the Race Course.[12] If one imagines a runner who must traverse the distance of a race course from the beginning, at point A, to the finish line, at point X, the runner must first traverse half of the course to the midpoint, at point B. Next, the runner must traverse half of the remaining distance, and then again and again. Each time, the runner covers only half the distance towards finishing the race course. If there are an infinite amount of intervals between points, then the runner could never reach the finish line. "The completion of an infinite sequence of acts in a finite time interval is logically impossible"[13] (Zeno, of course, did not believe in any extension of space or of time at all). The contradictions established through Zeno's arguments against motion have provided for philosophical debate and puzzlement throughout the centuries and continue to illustrate the paradox which arises between the actual performance of an act and the logical consideration of that act as a feature of a material reality.

An interesting mixture of monistic thinking presented within the context of a pluralistic framework can be seen in the rigorous dialectic of Plato (427-347 BC). While imparting what is arguably pluralistic ontology in his *Theory of Forms*, he nevertheless presented these archetypal blueprints against the backdrop of a unified transcendental reality. Although Plato rarely spoke of ultimate reality in other than mystical references one could see a direction in his philosophy that progressively synthesised the

---

[12] *The Encyclopedia of Philosophy*, Vol. VIII, 372-3.
[13] *The Encyclopedia of Philosophy*, Vol. VIII, 372.

dualistic features in the physical world toward higher singular precepts. A strong emphasis was placed on his belief in "degrees of reality"[14] and as the individual worked towards perceiving ever higher states of "the more real" so, too, did one come to see the essential *Forms* common to all things, and which conditioned the outer physical world. The final synthesis which would have made Plato's views substantially monistic were only hinted at, but never followed up thoroughly, in the *Republic*:

> ...in the intelligible world [the realm of the Forms] the last thing to be seen – and then only dimly – is the idea of the Good. Once seen, however, the conclusion becomes irresistible that *it* is the cause of all things right and good, that in the visible world *it* gives birth to light and its sovereign source, that in the intelligible world *it is itself* sovereign and the author of Truth and Reason...[15]

As we can see, Plato indicates that the highest state to be known – the idea of the *Good* – is, itself, the one creative eternal source, progenitor to the sun and author of "The Forms" in the intelligible realm. The passage shows the power of Plato's mystical vision and its durability to take us into an intelligible apprehension of our universe. In addition to this, we see how interpretations of pluralism and monism could

---

[14] Plato. *Republic*, translated by Richard W. Sterling and William C. Scott. (W. W. Norton and Company: New York, 1985) (507b-511e), 180-5. An example of the notion of "degrees of reality" can be found through Plato's use of the Line Analogy.
[15] Plato, (517b), 211.

co-exist as aspects in one overall outlook, sharing features of one comprehensive system of philosophical thought. Entering the period of Neoplatonism we find one of the greatest thinkers of the third century – namely, Plotinus (205-270 AD). As the founder of the first Neoplatonic school of thought, Plotinus adopted, yet built upon, many of the conceptions held by Plato. The transcendental reality hinted at by Plato became a centerpiece for Plotinus and sparked a renaissance of philosophical inquiry that fundamentally grounded a further 1500 years of Neoplatonism. His thoroughgoing convictions toward monism were born out of his rigorous education in Egypt and travels to Persia.[16] By the age of 20, this "mystic philosopher of saintly habits" moved to Rome where he lived and lectured for the rest of his life. The metaphysics of Plotinus posited a tripartite division of both the human being and the world as *body, soul* and *spirit. Spirit* existed as the divine aspect within the physical human being (*body*), and the *soul*, quasi-divine in essence, was able to function in both worlds and germinate an ever evolving conscious link between the two. Above all, though, he asserted the existence of the One as the highest principle encompassing all that is, and spent his life developing a coherent description of this view.[17] The One, considered as a necessary Being, was equivalent to spirit; with the sum total of

---

[16] M. M. Sharif. "Neoplatonism" *History of Philosophy Eastern and Western*, Vol. II Edited by Sarvepalli Radakrishnan. (Unwin Brothers Ltd.: London, 1953), 93.
[17] *The Encyclopedia of Philosophy*, Vol. VI, 353.

particular human spirits comprising the Universal Spirit. In this view, the Universal Spirit *was* the collective of all particular spirits in totality. All were Universal Spirit in potentiality.[18] An "emanation" or "effulguration" of each particular spirit demonstrated as the soul which, in its turn, was an emanating cause for the body. The soul provided a "divine link" between that which humans believed themselves to be (i.e., body) and that which humans were thought to be in essence (i.e., spirit) – yet of which they were still struggling to become aware. The journey back to spirit required a progressive understanding and awareness provided through the soul's ability to experience both poles of the One reality – *matter* and *spirit*. Based on these principles, a "cosmic sympathy" could be said to exist within the One Universal Being; each part affected, and was affected by, all other parts. As growth and awareness occurred for the individual, the pluralist experience of the world, as separate objects and forms, was eventually to be unified through its highest aspect, the "Absolute One" or "God". This he identified with Plato's *Form of the Good*. "Thus, according to Plotinus, the good of everything lays in its ascent, stage by stage, to the world yonder, the other world, the world of spirit, and even beyond, to the absolute unity of the One – its original source."[19] Neoplatonism, under the original insights of Plotinus, continued in some form or another up until the nineteenth century although it underwent many changes due to the influence of Aristotelian thought. Nevertheless,

---

[18] Sharif, 98.
[19] Sahrif, 101.

the doctrine of Plotinus powerfully introduced the notion of monism into the history of Western philosophy and went on to affect the succeeding meditations of many theists, philosophers and scientists. The medieval period in philosophy offered new approaches to monism. As a theologian more than philosopher, John Duns Scotus (c. 1266-1308 AD) sought answers to theological questions through the use of logic. The result of his work was, as a consequence, highly supportive of an ultimate view of the universe in monistic terms. Working on the problem of *transcendentals*, Scotus argued that, while it may be impossible to trace back through the causal chain of events that lead to an event from some primary cause, one could assert that whatsoever the true cause of any event happened to be, "it must coexist with and conserve the *effect* and therefore must be distinguished from the ancillary chain of partial causes that succeed one another in time."[20] His method of approach to identify the transcendental features involved the use of what he called *disjunctive attributes* (i.e., finite-or-infinite, necessary-or-contingent, cause-or-caused).

> In the disjunctive attributes, while the entire disjunction cannot be demonstrated from 'Being', nevertheless, as a universal rule, by positing the less perfect extreme of some Being, we can conclude that the more perfect extreme is realised in some other Being. Thus it follows that if some Being is finite, then some Being is infinite, and if some Being is contingent, then some Being is necessary. For in such cases it is not possible for

[20] *The Encyclopedia of Philosophy, Vol. II*, 429.

the more imperfect extreme of the disjunction to be existentially predicated of 'Being' particularly taken, unless the more perfect extreme be existentially verified of some other Being upon which it depends. (Ordinatio I, 39)[21]

In essence, one effectual extreme of the disjunction cannot be asserted without also asserting the other causal extreme of the disjunction. An important conclusion that follows from this *Law of Disjunction* is that: "There is one, and only one, Being in which all pure perfection exists. Such an infinite Being we call God."[22] Scotus, however, downplayed those conclusions in relation to what he felt to be of more practical importance – loving that Being. The latter became an essential consequence from proving the former. For all his contributions to both religion and philosophy, Scotus offered an interesting and important perspective on the idea of a monistic universe.

Events of the 17th century brought a significant turn to investigations in philosophy. New discoveries in science motivated serious reassessments of objects in the material world. Galileo's excitement with the idea of the atom heavily influenced others, like Newton, to decipher the dynamics found in the natural world. This opened a contentious rift between science and religion with a subsequent split in doctrinal approaches. Science became deeply rooted in the empirical study of natural objects and, for the most part, discarded the mystical approach as unreliable, obscure and fallible. Sir Isaac Newton's revival of complete commitment

---

[21] *The Encyclopedia of Philosophy, Vol. II*, 428-429.
[22] *The Encyclopedia of Philosophy, Vol. II*, 429.

to a pluralistic universe, composed of masses of atoms, encouraged a return to the Atomist's contentions of some early Greek thinkers. In light of this growing shift towards pluralism, the defenders of monism required a new and innovative approach in order to solve the ontological and epistemological questions raised by science.

Benedict Spinoza (1632-1677), a rationalist metaphysician from Amsterdam, was compelled to do just that in response to the mechanistic rationalism of French philosopher Rene Descartes who, in his own turn, had sought to understand the human being apart from its place in nature as a whole. Spinoza saw this view as epistemologically flawed and asserted that we could only grasp the nature of the part (i.e., the human being) once we understood the system as a whole first. To substantiate his claims, he developed an idiosyncratic deductive system, influenced by Euclid, to show that all truth statements presented by him could be seen as naturally connecting to, and derived from, other truth statements, axioms and propositions. This unique approach, offered through his highly rationalist system, was to link the concepts of *causality* and *essence*. Spinoza divided the properties of objects into those that were essential (necessary) and those that were accidental (contingent). Pursuing this notion, he inferred that the essential properties of a substance would provide not only an explanation into the essence of that object, but also the cause of that object. This followed from the proposition that:

...the cause of any being is that which not only brings that being into existence but also makes that being what it is and not another thing. Not only does the cause of a being make that being what it is, it also necessarily produces the effect that it does.[23]

This method of derivation brought Spinoza to conclude that there could exist only one necessary essential substance which was the cause of all things in and of itself. He inferred that the notions of "God" and "Nature" were actually the same thing; God did not make nature, God *was* nature; infinite and immanent. Additionally, Spinoza could provide an account for plurality in that, while there could only be one substance, there could be an infinite range of attributes. However, the actual transition in physics from the one to the many was difficult to understand in Spinoza's writing – and impossible to grasp given the scientific knowledge of that era. This, in combination with his denial of some of the fundamental views about Creation, left Spinoza in poor favour with the religious orthodoxy. Nevertheless, his contributions to moral, religious and political philosophy served as a staunch reminder that monism could be removed from the sphere of mysticism, described through a highly rational system, and employed to generate coherent responses to practical epistemological and ontological questions.

The rise of Empiricism ensued with the publication of Newton's *Philosophiae Naturalis Principia Mathematica* (1687). Through it he mounted a significant assault against monism by providing a stringent explanatory model for

---

[23] *The Encyclopedia of Philosophy, Vol. VII,* 532.

characterizing the many interactions and external relations between material objects. A tendency towards pluralism was seen in the works of Locke, Berkeley, Hume, Mill and Russell. Principles and arguments supporting pluralism rose in popularity. One of the stronger arguments for pluralistic individualism was advanced by Immanuel Kant in his philosophical masterpiece *Critique of Pure Reason* (1781). Working from the rationalist theories of Descartes and Leibniz, as well as the Empiricism of the British philosophers, Kant argued for the *Transcendental Unity of Apperception.* He looked at the Empiricist's assertions of the need for knowledge to conform to objects and, reversing this position, questioned instead whether our perception of objects might conform to our knowledge. Simply put, there can be "no connection or unity of one item of knowledge with another, without that unity of [internal] consciousness which precedes all data of intuitions, and by relation to which representation of objects is alone possible."[24] For Kant, this "perceptual unity of consciousness" demonstrated an original and necessary autonomy for consciousness in providing for self identity. This proposal was said to be verifiable by what appeared to be a conscious experience of a synthetic unity to the external appearance of objects. Taking this consideration in hand and, within his pluralistic view of the world, Kant begged the question that an individual necessarily required a unified identity of Self in order to coherently experience the world.

---

[24] *The Encyclopedia of Philosophy*, Vol. IV, 312.

A monistic view, however, might have easily thrown this claim into question as in, for example, the *Parable of the Whispering Trees* developed by John King-Farlow.[25] Undercutting through several dogmatic and anthropocentric perspectives found within some linguistic circles, King-Farlow demonstrated how there could be linguistic beings – those able to communicate coherently about objects in their environment – that lacked any formal concept of a separate Self or Self-identity.[26] A variation on this theme can also be drawn from his portrayal of a speaker-of-language's use of a monistic language. Viewing the world of forms as simple attributes or projections of the One, he offered the linguistic paradigm of "IT-ish" as a vehicle to accommodate language beings who held a nondual and non-self-separate perspective. Rather than using the names of things (nouns) objects were described with adjectives, verbs or adverbs in order to represent them as merely representing qualities or features of the one underlying "IT". For example, "John" became "John-like" (suggesting that some part of "IT" was arising or appearing "John-like") and "happy" became "happy-wise" (suggesting that "IT" was, at that moment, appearing "happy-wise"). All in all, there is only "IT" and entities that understood their appearance to be only an aspect of the underlying "IT" used language which would express that truth accurately.

---

[25] John King-Farlow, *Self-Knowledge and Social Relations*. (Science History Publications: New York, 1978), 84-96.
[26] King-Farlow, 108-114.

The previous two examples provide only a few exceptions to Kant's *Transcendental Unity of Apperception* and offer insights into how strict pluralist thinking could lead to contradictions in *a priori* deductions. Contradictions, however, need not serve as an end to philosophical propositions but may, in fact, provide the grounds for new propositions. Contradiction was embraced in the works of the German Idealist philosopher Georg Wilhelm Friedrich Hegel (1770-1831) and indicated a pathway on which Reason might comprehend the Absolute. The world of finite sensible things were, in Hegel's mind, not contradictory to each other but, rather, to the infinite. Therefore, any true philosophical system would need to explain the cause of that contradiction while maintaining an account of their existence. Utilizing a system of dialectic triads comprising *thesis, antithesis* and *synthesis*, Hegel sought to build upon a succession of contradictory notions to complete a picture of a quantitative monistic world while maintaining a justification for the practical experience of material pluralism. For Hegel, only *Mind*, or the *Absolute Idea*, was real and manifested itself in art, religion or socio-political movements as "a system of individual minds actively developing their potentialities by embodying them in increasingly complex forms."[27] The historical movement of human development was an elaborately detailed depiction of the contradictory manifestation of Infinite Being (antithesis), in finite material expression (thesis), in the process of *progressively* reconciling the interaction of those

---

[27] *The Encyclopedia of Philosophy, Vol. III*, 436.

contradictory notions (synthesis). Finite material manifestation – in other words, nature – appears as a distinct contradiction in relation to any notion of an Infinite Being and yet, for Hegel, God and nature meant the same thing; only appearing as contradictory because of the perspectives of individual minds located in any particular point in history. The progressive achievements throughout the history of mankind, seen as a whole, served as the increasingly complete expression of Absolute Spirit toward bridging this seemingly inherent contradiction. The true philosopher was one in which the contradictions were overcome whilst retaining a place for those contradictions to exist.

> ...there are [in Hegel's *Encyclopedia*] statements which say that the *Idea* decides to allow nature to go forth freely from itself (sec. 244), that 'nature has come to pass as the *Idea* in the form of otherness' (sec. 247), and that nature is 'the unresolved contradiction' (sec. 248).[28]

Being is not distinct from what is finite but is necessarily manifested in it. This unique system of logic provided Hegel the means to synthesize seemingly incompatible thoughts about reality and profoundly affected the future of philosophy. His complex and penetrating insights, covered only superficially here, instigated both an entirely new school of thought as well as invoking a backlash from critics re-asserting the virtues of Empiricism, Pragmatism, Atomism, Positivism and, in an unfortunate manner, dogmatic Pluralism.

---

[28] *The Encyclopedia of Philosophy, Vol. III*, 440.

In an attempt to offset this tendency toward a revival of British Empiricism, F. H. Bradley (1846-1924), an independent and original Idealist thinker, defended the monistic viewpoint by advancing on the foundations laid previously by Hegel. Bradley's most notable ideas were contained in his well-known work, *Appearance and Reality*.[29] Bradley delved into the self-contradicting character of mere appearances, and went on to defend the Absolute later in that famous book. Utilizing his insights into questions about traditional logic, Bradley criticized most branches of logic as inadequate for approaching true knowledge. His claim asserted that subject-predicate methods in formal logic omitted relational judgments and that knowledge could not advance from particulars to universals, nor from particulars to particulars, but could only be known on the basis of an understanding of the universals themselves. In other words, "both premises and conclusions must be organized around the central concept in a system of related concepts."[30] His argument involved a demonstration, in logical analysis, illustrating the self-contradictory status of external relations. In considering the relationships between all things as groups of related attributes, Bradley argued:

> ...that if A and B stand in relation to C, then C must be related to A and B by *another* relation D, and this by a third relation E, and so on indefinitely...if simple qualities are to be conceived, they must be conceived as related to one another; but if A is related to B, then there must be the

---

[29] Richard Wollheim, *F. H. Bradley*. (Penguin Books: Hammondsworth, Middlesex, 1959).
[30] *The Encyclopedia of Philosophy*, Vol. *I*, 361.

independent aspect of A and the aspect in which it is related to B must be related to one another, so that there is set up in each of them a further plurality of aspects generating...'a principle of fission which conducts us to no end'.[31]

This infinite regress occurs if one considers the world as a plurality of independent autonomous objects, for such regress can only lead to the conclusion that "plurality and relatedness are but features and aspects of unity."[32] Additionally, Bradley pointed out the contradictory nature in our thinking about external objects.

> Wherever there is thought, there is the distinction between the *what* and the *that*, between ideal content and reality, between adjective and substantive; and hence wherever there is thought, there is contradiction.[33]

Seen in this light, a contradiction exists in our mental conceptions of things by viewing the "adjectival" properties as something distinct from the object itself. Likewise, to hold a mental image of objects as separate from each other creates a contradictory view of the world itself as a whole. To exhibit a coherent state of reality, there must exist one underlying unity upon which all those appearances rely. This denies individual autonomy to such notions as space, time, causation, the Self, or "things" since they all imply self-contradicting relations. Bradley was to conclude in his main *Anti-Relational Argument*

---

[31] *The Encyclopedia of Philosophy, Vol. I.* 361.
[32] *The Encyclopedia of Philosophy, Vol. I,* 362.
[33] *The Encyclopedia of Philosophy, Vol. I,* 362.

that the notion of any relation, whether internal or external, would result in either an infinite regress or a self-contradiction. The implication of his argument was that pluralism is logically incoherent.

Bradley went on to argue that Reality, by virtue of its very existence, could not have discord or inconsistency within itself. In fact, he assigns two positive attributes to Reality in order to ensure its self-consistency and self-sufficiency: *Individuality* and *Perfection*. To ascribe *Individuality* to Reality is to say that, as one unified whole, it has extension (i.e., completeness) and harmony; a distinctive unity wherein its elements cohere to form a whole, and a completeness that is unrestricted by any potential external imposition by some other Individual. Therefore, harmony, of necessity, demands completeness and these attributes, also of necessity, require that Reality must be *One Individual* in order for it to exist coherently at all. Likewise, the attribute of *Perfection* demands harmony (by definition) as well as unrestricted extension. This unrestricted extension, taken once again to mean completeness, provides that if A (i.e., a perfect Being) were placed beside B (i.e., another perfect Being) the very relationship of one to the other would produce a dependence on one another for identity that would eliminate *independent* Individuality. From this, the internal harmony or unity within each Individual would cease to exist unless those objects merged into a larger entity AB and, thus, restored Individuality. Harmony is then regained internally providing a coherent experience of the world. From this, Bradley argued that the universe, as *One Individual*, must be monistic.

Bradley's philosophical conclusions made a profound impact on British philosophy but fell out of favour institutionally. This was due mainly to the anti-metaphysical tendencies of the twentieth century, as well as a harsh reaction to German and neo-Hegelian ideas after 1914. The mainstream defenders of dogmatic Scientism and institutionalized Materialism attacked Bradley's sophisticated arguments with oafish tenacity. Bradley's arguments for monism were swiftly assaulted by noted philosophers like Bertrand Russell in his *Doctrine of External Relations*. In his essay on *Logical Atomism* (1924), Russell asserted that "a relational proposition is not, in general, logically equivalent formally to one or more subject-predicate propositions."[34] This assertion, denying Bradley's analysis based on type distinctions, led to a further rejection of monism. But despite his dogmatic attachment to pluralism, even Russell admitted doubts about his own use of formal logic to provide answers to this question.

> If I am right [in the difficulties of relating the languages of Logic and Epistemology], there is nothing in Logic that can help us to decide between monism and pluralism, or between the view that there are ultimate relational facts and the view that there are none. My own decision in favour of pluralism and relations is taken on *empirical grounds* [emphasis mine], after convincing myself that the *a priori* arguments to the contrary are valid.[35]

---

[34] Bertrand Russell. *Logical Atomism*. (Unwin Brothers Limited: London, 1956), 335.
[35] Russell, 338-339.

Russell's honesty revealed his own empiricist bias as providing, perhaps, the only real source of conviction about pluralism. Unfortunately for Russell, empiricism goes with the 'givens' of human *experience* – despite the fact that human experience relies upon the physical senses and is, by definition, pluralistic and dualistic in its perception of the world. In the end, Russell is content to rely on empirical science and surrender to the belief that "the risk of error in philosophy is pretty sure to be greater than in science."[36] Russell, like so many of his mainstream contemporaries, merely grounded his pluralist convictions in a simple *method of inquiry* – namely, science – which, for the most part, had unquestioningly derived many of its conclusions under the original assumptions of a pluralist paradigm. Russell had no sooner staked his philosophical claims on scientific empiricism than when the first murmurs of quantum physics began to surface; the implications of which were to later shatter our empirical notions regarding the material world.

There seems to be a rebirth and renaissance in the current decades surrounding the idea of monism and nondualism. Science, in the latter half of the 20th century, made several startling discoveries that not only hinted at but, in many ways, demonstrated a monistic conception of the universe. New secrets in nature are slowly revealing themselves, providing unique insights in-accessible to earlier philosophers. As a primary axiom in physics, science now states that everything we perceive of the known universe is *energy* in some attributive

---

[36] Russell, 339.

appearance or another. While our sensual experience of the world registers within one narrow aspect of that energetic interplay – the physical world – we are, in fact, immersed in an ocean of energies at both the atomic and subatomic level. We are constantly participating in exchanges with those energies which are involved in establishing the patterns cognitively recorded by our sensory equipment. In a metaphorical sense, we are no more separate from this great sea of energy than a drop of water is from the ocean.

No less striking are statements issued by some quantum physicists who try to reach the public with their message of universal oneness. David Z. Albert, professor of philosophy at Columbia University, gives us a hint at the changing face of physics:

> What needs to be changed [as a result of quantum physics] is the fundamental ontology of the world. What you have to do is give up the idea that the material world consists of particles...[37]

This statement presents a clear challenge to thinkers in every field whose conception of reality is still rooted in materialist conceptions of the world. Amit Goswami, professor of physics at the Institute of Theoretical Sciences at the University of Oregon, expands upon that challenge in the following way:

> The alternative that I propose... is *monistic idealism*.... This philosophy posits that everything

---

[37] David Z. Albert. *Quantum Mechanics and Experience.* (Harvard University Press: Cambridge, 1992), 59.

(including matter) exists in and is manipulated from consciousness. Note that [it] does not say that matter is unreal but that the reality of matter is secondary to that of consciousness, which itself is the ground of all being – including matter...monistic idealism provides a paradox-free interpretation of quantum physics that is logical, coherent, and satisfying. Moreover, mental phenomena – such as self-consciousness, free will, creativity, even extrasensory perception – find simple, satisfying explanations when the mind-body problem is reformulated in an overall context of monistic idealism and quantum theory.[38]

This notion is equally reflected in statements made by Professor Henry P. Stapp, Lawrence Berkeley Laboratory, University of California:

> The image of man described above places human consciousness in the inner workings of a non-local global process that links the whole universe together in a manner totally foreign to both classical physics and the observation of everyday life. If the world indeed operates in the way suggested by Heisenberg's ontology then we are all integrally connected in some not-yet-fully-understood global process that is actively creating the form of the universe...
> Science recognizes no authority whose *ex cathedra* pronouncements can be claimed to express a divine will. Nevertheless, this new conception of the universe emphasizes an intricate and profound global wholeness and it gives man's consciousness a creative, dynamical, and integrating role in the intrinsically global

---

[38] Amit Goswami, *The Self-Aware Universe: How Consciousness Creates the Material World.* (Tarcher/Putnam: New York, 1993), 10-11.

process that forms the world around us.... Implicit in this conceptual shift in man's perception of his relationship to the rest of nature is the foundation of a new ethics, one that would conceive the 'self' of self-interest very broadly, in a way that would include in appropriate measure all life on our planet.[39]

While their statements remain yet to be fully proven, we can see that – at least in the thoughts of some quantum physicists – monism has resurfaced once again to provide a coherent explanation for universal phenomena. Certainly, not all quantum physicists agree on the interpretation of their work. Many ideas forged at the frontiers of the new physics press painfully against the materialist's notion of the universe. Perhaps our best approach, then, can be summed up in the words of Amit Goswami:

> The axioms of material realism – materialism, determinism, locality, and so forth – served us well in the past when our knowledge was more limited than it is today, but now they have become our trap. We may have to let go of the chickpeas of certainty in order to embrace the freedom that lies outside the material arena.[40]

What is required of us all at this time is a return to that state of eager inquiry and a willingness to surrender our cynicism and destructive criticism. Ideology has no place in the laboratory if we are to uncover those pathways which could lead us to the new world.

---

[39] Henry P. Stapp. *Mind, Matter, and Quantum Mechanics.* (Springer-Verlag: New York, 1993), 214.
[40] Goswami, 47.

This exploration of western monism shows that the notion of nonduality is more widespread than what, perhaps, many realise. Moreover, I have hoped to illustrate that, far from being ineffable, monism can be presented through ideas available to all. While nonduality can sometimes be daunting – given its counter-intuitive nature – it remains logically coherent in every challenge and provides one of the most rational and robust explanations for reality. Arguments against nonduality and monism, particularly in the west, seem most often due to a type of reactive hostility grounded within an unsubstantiated rejection of mysticism and spirituality. But there is nothing in analytical or logical philosophy itself that precludes monism. It is only when analysis and logic are buried in dogmatic Scientism and Naturalism that you find a break between analytical philosophy and monism. In the west, attacks on monism have been based largely on false premises coupled with philistine narrow-mindedness. What we have seen, however, is that monism is a significant topic in philosophy necessitating a serious treatment of it on the part of philosophers. Having withstood the tests of time and rigorous analysis the ideas found in monism are stronger now than ever before and it is my hope that this essay has evoked from the reader a new interest in this fascinating doctrine.

I've described some thinkers who are often accepted as monists. They range from the beginnings of western philosophy in Greece and extend through the 20th century. The major part of this essay has been given to presenting, in a brief manner, the thoughts of some leading western monists. I have endeavoured to assert that monism should be taken more seriously – not only by academics and theorists of all fields but in every aspect of our lives. Towards that end I offer the following further consideration.

Philosophers are seen to be the heirs of cultural history, explorers of moral truth and "lovers of wisdom" for its own sake. They shouldn't be seen as bound to philistine narrow-mindedness within the rigid boundaries of institutional dogmatism or vocational egotism. The traditions of Materialism, Empiricism and Dualism have dominated much of the historical development of philosophy and science in the west. At the same time we have seen that there is no shortage of defendants for nondualism and monism. Monism, therefore, shares with those former views a reputation of *historical adequacy*. No shortage of accounts can be found, in both quality and variety, to argue for the efficacy of monism; and are contained in the meditations of some of the most respected and lucid minds in history. On the shoulders of these pioneers stands the whole tradition of philosophical inquiry as well as its contributions to cultural development. A failure even to attempt to uphold the historical importance and logical coherence of monism as an equal amongst the other major categories strips philosophy of its rigorous objectivity and social relevance. Seen in this light, the monistic perspective offers a significant challenge to western philosophers, not least of which has been a willingness to provide serious answers to some of the leading social, economic and political issues of this century.

When philosophy ceases to be in touch with the history of human culture then something can be said to have gone drastically wrong. If monism is to suffer neglect in the hands of our "seekers of truth" then philosophy will be tearing up its own roots. If a life of philosophy is a life worth living, it is so because of what it can contribute to *society and culture*. One would hope that philosophy could continue to provide succour to present and future generations without falling prey to indifference to its own past.

Nonduality and the Sufi Tradition[1]

> It is not the body, nor the personality that is the true self. The true self is eternal. Even on the point of death we can say to ourselves, "my true self is free. I cannot be contained.
> —*Marcus Aurelius*

The major western religious traditions, in sharing both history and primary texts, have demonstrated great parallels with regard to their outer or exoteric doctrine and that aspect which is considered the inner esoteric path. For Judaism we have the esoteric doctrine of Kabbalah. Christianity offers its own mystical traditions including Hermetic Christianity and several forms of monasticism. Islam, too, contains a similar esoteric tradition – Sufism – and it has had the reputation of producing some of the most celebrated masters in esotericism. Like its mystical traditions in other religions, Sufism has suffered condemnation from its orthodox parent and has often served as a point of contention for those adhering to mainstream views of Islam. One wonders what mysteries arise from within Sufism to create such an apparent and distinct threat to the monotheistic foundations of Islamic orthodoxy?

The former Spalding Professor of Eastern Religions and Ethics at the University of Oxford, R. C. Zaehner, explains that "in Sufism the tendency is from theism, that is, a mysticism of

---

[1] First published as "Monism and the Sufi Tradition" *Axis Mundi.* Nov/2000. (ISSN 1496-2578) and has been revised, updated and re-edited for this book.

love, towards what amounts to monism in that, in the states called *fana* ('annihilation') and *infirad* ('isolation'), it is claimed that there is no consciousness of anything but God, man thereby realizing himself as God."[2] One can certainly see the initial polarisation that might occur between monism's 'God Immanent' and Islam's monotheistic view of 'God Transcendent'. Sufism, as a whole, does not adopt this view lightly and the "claims that at the height of his mystical experience man actually *is* God, is frequently challenged by the Sufis themselves."[3] Within its own circle Sufism has not had to provide proof for its claims. Conviction is based upon direct inner experience. However, these claims are often considered heretical since they lack any formally accepted tenets to substantiate them and where the Sufi claims of equality with God seem to turn the notion of 'submission to God' on it head.[4] For this reason, Sufi practitioners have been subjected to a long history of rejection, isolation and even martyrdom. The Qur'an has sometimes been presented by mainstream Muslims as the progenitor of many discoveries in classical science. Is it possible then that the subtle notions in Sufism may, likewise, play a similar role with regard to a subtler side of new sciences such as quantum mechanics?

In this essay I will provide a general look at the doctrines of some of the great Sufi masters in

---

[2] R. C. Zaehner, *Hindu and Muslim Mysticism.* (Rockport: Oneworld Publications, 1994), 11-12.
[3] Zaehner, 12.
[4] "Islam" comes from the Arabic root *islām* meaning 'submission', or from the Arabic *aslama* meaning 'submit (to the will of God)'.

order to identify the thread of nonduality running through them. Following this, I will provide some evidence from modern science, specifically quantum physics, which suggests that the monistic conceptions in Sufism may, in fact, find a degree of substantiation within the scientific community. From this it will be seen that the claims of Sufis throughout history cannot be dismissed so easily by the Islamic orthodoxy and may even provide insights toward the advance of science.

Running deep within the Sufi tradition is the notion of oneness *with* God. The fundamental monotheistic Islamic notion of *Tawhid* ("making God one") was pursued most vigorously by such early Sufi adherents as Al-Junayd (d. 910). While he maintained that there must always remain some distinction between God and His creation, nevertheless, he felt that one could unite temporarily and experience oneself as within the Perfection of God. This mystical state could be achieved by incurring a complete denial of the self and the physical world, and this pursuit eventually led to the "development of the central Sufi doctrine of *fana*"[5] (from Arabic meaning 'annihilation').[6] The insistence, in Al-Junayd's 'sober' form of Sufism, in maintaining a distinction between God and creation was not favourable to all Sufi practitioners and some of his contemporaries pursued an 'intoxicated' form

---

[5] Frederick Mathewson Denny, *An Introduction to Islam* (New York: Macmillan Publishing Company, 1994), 232.
[6] It is interesting to note the similarity between the Sufi mystical term *fana*, meaning "annihilation", and the Buddhist mystical term *nirvana*, also meaning "annihilation".

of Sufism which exemplified an even more extreme position within the tradition. Abu Yazid al-Bistami (d. 875) went so far as to acknowledge the living presence of God within himself. His most controversial proclamations – including "Glory to Me! How great is My Majesty!"[7] and "I am He"[8] – spoke to his absolute identification with God. While this vision invoked a great deal of censure, none seemed quite so disagreeable to the orthodox authorities as Al-Junayd's infamous disciple, Husayn Ibn Mansur Al-Hallaj (d. 922). Frederick Denny recounts the profound, yet tragic, events of Al-Hallaj's life and message:

> His most famous utterance and the one that, because he refused to recant it, cost him his life, was *ana al-Haqq*, 'I am God' (literally, 'I am Truth' or 'Reality'). Another thing that caused him great trouble was his claim to have miraculous powers. Others accused him of magic. This strange mystic became the most extreme of the intoxicated Sufis, identifying absolutely with God, his beloved.... In 922, Hallaj was crucified in Baghdad for his blasphemy.[9]

His slow and excruciatingly painful execution was endured with absolute courage and history records that he did not plead for pardon once. In fact, his ecstatic experience of identification with God allowed him to plead for forgiveness for his captors at the outset of his execution.

---

[7] A. J. Arberry, *Sufism* (New York: Harper Torchbooks, 1970), 54.
[8] Zaehner, 14.
[9] Denny, 237.

One very famous Muslim figure claimed by many to be second only to Muhammad[10] was Abu Hamid Muhammad Al-Ghazali (1058-1111). While his teachings were certainly Sufic in their support of mystical unification with God he retreated from the notion of complete union, although he maintained a clear respect for God's transcendence; a return to the notions forwarded earlier by Al-Junayd. Nevertheless, his contribution was great in its clear-minded critique of the limitations in academic knowledge. It was possible, he felt, to be completely learned in all subjects yet still lacking in true insight or knowledge. Idries Shah describes Al-Ghazali's perspective in this way,

> He insisted upon pointing out that those who are learned may be, and often are, stupid as well, and can be bigoted, obsessed. He affirms that, in addition to having information and being able to reproduce it, there is such a thing as knowledge, which happens to be a higher form of human thought.
> The habit of confusing opinion with knowledge, a habit which is to be met with every day at the current time, Ghazali regards as an epidemic disease.[11]

While Al-Ghazali retreats slightly from the full nondualistic notion of some earlier Sufis, he does, nevertheless, point out that the higher forms of knowledge are achieved beyond what is found in mere academic study. It is discovered only experientially and subjectively. This

---

[10] Denny, 240.
[11] Idries Shah, *The Way of the Sufi*. (London: Penguin Books, 1968), 56-57.

encouragement towards subjective experience served to reinforce the Sufi's inner subjective search for God.

The retreat from monism by Al-Ghazali was short lived with the arrival of Muhyiddin Ibn Al-Arabi (1165-1240) – considered one of the greatest Sufi Masters. According to Denny, Ibn Al-Arabi "brought Sufi thought to its highest point of subtlety and sophistication in his philosophy of *wahdat al-wujud* 'the oneness of being.'"[12] S.A.Q. Husaini notes that, in understanding the meaning of this term, the "one English word which can best represent this theory is 'monism.'"[13] However, because there can be many forms of monism, he would best associate the notions of Ibn-Arabi with pantheistic monism. That is, all finite things are regarded as,

> ...merely aspects, modifications, or parts of one eternal and self-existing being, which views all material objects and all particular minds as necessarily derived from a single infinite substance. The one absolute substance, the one all comprehensive being is called God. Thus God, according to it, is all that is, and nothing is which is not necessarily included in or which has not been evolved out of God.[14]

This clearly reflects the idea suggested by Ibn-Arabi. However, his notion of *wahdat al-wujud*, or 'oneness of being', is even more subtle than that. Annemarie Schimmel points out that there is no verb meaning *to be* in the Arabic

---

[12] Denney, 263.
[13] S.A.Q. Husaini, *The Pantheistic Monism of Ibn Al-Arabi.* (Lahore: Ashraf Press, 1970), viii.
[14] Husaini, viii.

language.[15] Instead, *wujud* suggests 'discovering' or 'unveiling'. As a result, Ibn-Arabi taught of the need to unveil, reveal or discover the Oneness of Reality. We see this in one of the many definitive statements from Ibn-Arabi's work, *The Fusus Al-Hikam.*

> For those who truly know *ahl al-haqaiq*, the Divine Realities, affirmation of transcendence imposes conditionality and limitation on the Real, for he who asserts that Deity is purely transcendent is either ignorant or tactless. The exorcist who stresses only Divine Transcendence (*at-tanzih*) slanders and misrepresents the Real and all the messengers, albeit unwittingly. He imagines that he has hit on the truth, whilst he has missed the mark, being like those who believe in part and deny part. It is known that the Scriptures express the Real as *shari'a*, traditional law, so that the generality of men grasp the apparent meaning. The elite, on the other hand, understand the meanings hidden in that utterance, regardless of the terms in which it is expressed. The truth is that the Real is manifest in every created being and in every concept, even whilst He is hidden from all understanding, save for one who recognises that the Cosmos is His form and Self, and who sees the world as the Divine Name, *az-zahir*, the Manifest. But He is also unmanifested Spirit, *al-batin*, the Unmanifest. In this sense He is, in relation to the manifested forms of the Cosmos, the Ruling Spirit.[16]

---

[15] Annemarie Schimmel, *Mystical Dimensions of Islam* (Chapel Hill: University of North Carolina Press, 1975), 59-62.
[16] Muhyiddin Ibn Al-Arabi, *The Seals Of Wisdom: From The Fusus Al-Hakim* ed. Raghavan Iyer. (London: Concord Grove Press, 1983), 47.

For Ibn-Arabi, there is nothing in the universe but God. In fact, the universe, and everything in it, *is* God.[17] Ibn-Arabi is again direct in his understanding of Reality and attempts to explain how God can be both immanent and transcendent at one and the same time.

> There is nothing in existence except God.... There is nothing except the unity of all things. There are no two things, and no distinction can be made.
> What is the meaning of the saying of the Prophet (may peace be on him): 'There is God and with Him?' The reply is this. Thingness cannot accompany Him, nor can it be attributed to Him. He remains as He is and nothing remains with Him. To be devoid of thingness and its company is His very attribute. Yet He is with, rather in, all things; but the things are not with Him, because company is dependent on knowledge. He knows us, so He is with us. But we do not know Him, so we are not with Him.[18]

For Ibn-Arabi, God is transcendent in the sense that we do not know Him as the source and foundation of ourselves. It is the Sufi master, one who has penetrated the barriers to this knowledge, that finally sees that the source, foundation and identity of oneself *is* God.

This notion is clearly explained by another well noted Sufi master and poet, Mawlana Jalal Al-Din Al-Rumi (ca. 1247-1273). Thought to be chief amongst the ecstatic poets, Rumi composed over 25,000 couplets in Persian during the course of his life. The subtlety of his thinking

---

[17] Husaini, 177.
[18] Husaini, 178-9.

mirrors that of Ibn-Arabi's and we can see this demonstrated in his discourse on Al-Hallaj's immortal phrase *Ana 'l-Haqq* ('I am God').

People imagine that it is a presumptuous claim, whereas it is really a presumptuous claim to say *Ana 'l-'abd* 'I am the slave of God'; and *Ana 'l-Haqq* 'I am God' is an expression of great humility. The man who says *Ana 'l-'abd* 'I am the slave of God' affirms two existences, his own and God's, but he that says *Ana 'l-Haqq* 'I am God' has made himself non-existent and has given himself up and says 'I am God', i.e. 'I am naught, He is all; there is no being but God's.' This is the extreme of humility and self-abasement.[19]

Rumi gracefully substantiates the profound sense of 'unity in the divine' expressed by many Sufi mystics before him. One is then considered to be at their greatest point of submission when in the Sufi state of total annihilation *(fana)*. For the Sufi, to attribute any notion of actual separation between God and creation is to be in a state of illusion as well as arrogance. To set oneself up, or affirm oneself as, an existence separate from God would be to claim a form of egocentric equivalence or individuality independent of God. That is, humans would represent something in the universe that was 'additional to' the presence of God.

We can see from the above examination that Sufism has, for the most part, posited a nondualistic conception of the world. When taken to its ultimate understanding, there can be

---

[19] Reynold A. Nicholson, *Rumi: Poet and Mystic (1207-1273: Selections from His Writings)*. (London: Allen & Unwin, 1950), 184.

nothing other than God and humans can only be a manifestation or emanation of God. Until recently, this notion was left to stand on logical reasoning alone and, perhaps, on the rare instance of pure subjective experience. As such, the Sufi adherents were vulnerable to condemnation by authorities not convinced by their postulates. However, science has recently added empirical evidence which suggests that the Sufi masters may, in fact, be expressing a deeper truth. This does not, in itself, reduce the validity or claims regarding the Sufi's inner experience of divinity. It does, however, provide a perspective through which to understand the Sufi claims for those who are not predisposed to grasping that experiential vision.

Quantum physics has offered science a fresh approach to viewing the universe. While it is far from answering all the secrets in the universe, there are certainly definitive claims available regarding previously held notions of the universe. David Z. Albert, Professor of Philosophy at Columbia University, describes some of these new fundamentals: "What needs to be changed is the fundamental ontology of the world. What you have to do is give up the idea that the material world consists of particles."[20] From the outset, this statement throws into question any claim from the perspective that we are solely material beings. While it does not substantiate, in itself, a monistic conception of the universe, it does undermine our common experience as separate material entities.

---

[20] David Z. Albert, *Quantum Mechanics and Experience* (Cambridge: Harvard University Press, 1992), 59.

In his book *The Self-Aware Universe*, Amit Goswami refers to the experiments by Alain Aspect in 1982 which evidenced a *transcendent* non-material domain of reality, known as the *non-local* domain, through which information from one material object (i.e., an atomic particle) could pass and affect the behaviour of another beyond the restrictions of time and space.[21] That is to say, this signal-less transmission of information could occur between objects instantaneously (faster than the speed of light) regardless of their location in space. As Goswami recounts,

> ...the message of quantum non-locality is that 'the fundamental process of Nature lies outside space-time but generates events that can be located in space-time.[22]

The generation of our *experience* of observed events is called 'the collapse of the wave function' and this collapse is instigated or affected through consciousness. In addition to this, the real work that the quantum theory does for us is that it completely opens a new line of thought regarding the causal powers of consciousness. To put this into a better perspective we might look at a conclusion related by Dr. Nick Herbert:

> In his [John von Neumann's] magisterial tome *The Mathematical Foundations of Quantum Physics*, regarded by many scientists as 'the bible of quantum theory,'... [he addressed the problem

---

[21] Amit Goswami, *The Self-Aware Universe: How Consciousness Creates the Material World*. (New York: Penguin Putnam, Inc., 1993), 117-21.
[22] Goswami, 61.

that] something new must be added to 'collapse the wave function,' something that is capable of turning fuzzy quantum possibilities into definite actualities [i.e., properties]. But since von Neumann is forced to describe the entire physical world as possibilities, the process that turns some of these maybes into actual facts cannot be a physical process.... Searching his mind for an appropriate actually existing nonphysical entity that could collapse the wave function, von Neumann reluctantly concluded that the only known entity fit for this task was *consciousness*. In von Neumann's interpretation, the world remains everywhere in a state of pure possibility except where some conscious mind decides to promote a portion of the world from its usual state of indefiniteness into a condition of actual existence.... By itself the physical world is not fully real, *but takes shape only as a result of the acts of numerous centers of consciousness.*[23]

This last statement is surprisingly parallel to the notions put forth by AIbn-Arabi in his pantheistic monism. According to von Neumann, it appears as though it is consciousness alone which is fit to collapse the wave function of the indiscriminate quantum field states into a material property state. [24] In fact, this may

---

[23] Nick Herbert, *Elemental Mind: Human Consciousness and the New Physics* (New York: Penguin Books, 1993), 155-6.

[24] The issue here is not *whether* the collapse occurs from a quantum state to a 'physical property' state. That has already been empirically proven. The difficulty presently concerning quantum physicists is one of determining exactly *when* the collapse actually occurs. For instance, does the collapse occur as the 'experiment' begins or does it occur when the final measured property of the experiment is registered as a

require that consciousness be a universal property, *sub-atomically* present in the field of each mathematical point in space, and not simply 'localized' to human brains – otherwise, the collapse of the wave function required to objectify our entire known universe would, ridiculously so, be the sole task of human minds. Consciousness, of which human beings are participants, plays an important role in creating the world.

This idea is mirrored in an interview with Dr. Larry Dossey, former Chief of Staff of Medical City Dallas Hospital.

> The non-local model [of mind] is...not confined in space and time to the brain and body, *it may work through the brain and body*.... Infinite, and by inference immortal, eternal, – all of these are consequences of anything that is non-local, not just mind. As a result, if mind is non-local, there is one mind, or Universal Mind, which is identical to what the West has regarded as Soul.... The evidence is overwhelming that mind behaves in a non-local way.... It may be hard to imagine, but physics experiments have *clearly* shown that non-locality is *the* characteristic of the world at the sub-atomic level.[25]

'mental state' in the observer? Answers to these questions, if they can even *be* answered, would bring us much closer to defining exactly the causal role that consciousness plays.

[25] Betsy Whitfill, "Interview with Dr. Larry Dossey: Recovering the Soul", *Share International* magazine. This statement was part of a conversation discussing the effects of prayer and positive thoughts in healing the body. Medical science has now had to admit, if only reluctantly, that the mind (i.e., consciousness)

So far, we have seen that quantum physics, as evidenced through empirical scientific investigation, validates a new paradigm: "that consciousness, not matter, is the ground of all being."[26] Amit Goswami, professor of physics at the Institute of Theoretical Sciences at the University of Oregon, feels that,

> ...the philosophy of monistic idealism provides a paradox-free interpretation of quantum physics that is logical, coherent, and satisfying. Moreover, mental phenomena – such as self consciousness, free will, creativity, even extrasensory perception – find simple, satisfying explanations when the mind-body problem is reformulated in an overall context of monistic idealism and quantum theory. This reformulated picture of the mind-brain enables us to understand our whole self entirely in harmony with what the great spiritual traditions have maintained for millennia.[27]

Goswami goes on to provide a description of how the universe consists as One whole field of consciousness, unlimited, unbroken and eternal. This same consciousness is experienced individually through the material physical vehicle we describe as the body and brain. It is this *experience*, however, which is the illusion and, as the Sufi masters would assert, one needs to penetrate deeply – beyond one's own illusory separate identity – to experience oneself as this underlying whole field of Oneness Consciousness. Other physicists in the field, including

---

plays a fundamental role in our quality of physical health.
[26] Goswami, *Self-Aware*, 2.
[27] Goswami, 11.

such well known names as Stapp,[28] Bohm,[29] and Capra[30] offer similar, if not identical, views of the universe. While they may differ slightly in the details, they all agree that a nondual conception of the universe is empirically undeniable. It is also fair to mention that, as was the case within the orthodoxy of Islam, not all in the community of Classical Physics share these ideas.

Others are attempting to solve the problems of physics based on dualistic or materialistic views of reality. To date, however, monistic theories have consistently provided the most coherent systems of thought and a more thorough examination of quantum physics is beyond the scope of this essay. To that we can add that nonduality deserves a great deal of consideration if we recognise that this approach to viewing the world is also the view set out by mystics throughout the ages as their *actual* experience of Reality. In a rare occasion, we are

---

[28] Henry P. Stapp, *Mind, Matter, and Quantum Physics*. (New York: Springer-Verlag, 1993). Henry Stapp provides a powerful model to explain how the quantum field interacts with the brain of individuals. He develops his model in part by combining concepts from Heisenberg and William James.

[29] David Bohm, *Wholeness and the Implicate Order* (London: Routledge & Kegan Paul, 1980). Bohm is a well-known and highly respected quantum physicist who participated in several memorable conversations with J. Krishnamurti on the nature of mind and consciousness.

[30] Fritjof Capra, *The Tao of Physics: An Exploration of the Parallels Between Modern Physics and Eastern Mysticism* (London: HarperCollins Publishers, 1982). Fritjof Capra was one of the early pioneers to make detailed comparisons between quantum physics and Eastern mysticism.

seeing science and religion (more specifically, mysticism) agreeing on a fundamental view of the universe. One would think that this in itself would be cause for celebration.

In conclusion, I have shown how some central figures in the Sufi tradition have put forward the concept of a monistic universe. For this, many have paid a dear price – including, at times, their own lives. Further, I have shown that this view of a monistic universe is likewise becoming popular for some within the scientific community. Based on recent experiments, science is now able to definitively claim that matter and the physical world are merely secondary features of the universe. The true foundation, it is believed, lies in an underlying omniscient field of consciousness which animates – and is even responsible for – the formation of the material world. This underlying field, or as it has been tentatively described by some mystics as 'God' – can be accessed if individuals could seek to transcend their own illusory sense of a separate self. This notion is completely in line with the teachings of the great Sufi Masters and the lines between these apparently different fields are rapidly blurring. The transcendent experience, attested to by the Sufi mystic is that great mystical experience described as the 'Union with God.' That science is possibly on the verge of discovering aspects of this Reality marks a great time for humanity. Now, more so than ever, is it incumbent upon all to join hands in this search, mystics and scientists alike, to understand our place in the universe.

A Challenge to Critical Theory and Cultural Studies from Nonduality[1]

> We dream that we are awake, we dream that we are asleep. The three states are only varieties of the dream state. Treating everything as a dream liberates. As long as you give reality to dreams, you are their slave. By imagining that you are born as so and so, you become a slave to the so-and-so. The essence of slavery is to imagine yourself to be a process, to have past and future, to have history.
> —*Sri Nisargadatta Maharaj*

The canon of Critical Theory contains a storehouse of analytical and discursive texts from an assortment of diverse perspectives. This field is traditionally defined as a philosophical approach to culture – and especially to language and literature – which seeks to analyze and confront those historical or ideological forces behind the development of culture. Critical Theory is commonly oriented toward critiquing and changing society by challenging the social, historical and ideological structures that produce and define society. This field is populated by works from such celebrated authors as Herbert Marcuse, Theodor Adorno, Jurgen Habermas, Max Horkheimer, Walter Benjamin and Eric Fromm, to name a few. However, despite this

---

[1] This article was first published in *Crossing Boundaries*. Volume 2, Issue 1. Apr/2002 and has been revised, updated and re-edited for this book.

diversity of viewpoints, a type of myopia exists which has plagued the mainstream of Critical Theory. This bias, for whatever social or cultural reasons, has tended to discriminate against the inclusion of any significant *nondual* theories as tools for examining or critiquing the foundations of cultural construction. Writers such as Whitehead (1978), Bradley (1978), or Hegel (1977) are only a few of those scholars whose penetrating insights on nonduality have found their way into the canon of accepted teaching and, yet, little attention has been paid to examining the constructs of society and culture through this immensely important lens. In the east, there are countless authors across many traditions espousing nondual doctrines including Taoism, Advaita Vedanta, and the Buddhist concept of *Anātman* – otherwise known as the doctrine of 'no-self'. This latter theory on *Anātman*, which asserts that belief in a distinct self-existent identity is an illusion, provides a lucid and challenging account on identity theory unparalleled in western circles. In fact, it contains a robust rational scheme having few historical challenges to its conclusions.

Nevertheless, the doctrine of *Anātman* remains relatively absent from the mainstream of western cultural studies and social theory. As Whitehead once correctly suggested, conclusive theories such as these are rarely challenged but, rather, are ignored. Until recently, cultural studies in the west appear to have been successful in ignoring the concepts of 'non-identity' in Buddhist *Anātman* (as well as much of the eastern theories on 'self' and 'identity') and have lived within the boundaries of their own self-imposed dualistic framework – seemingly unsure of how to face the challenges put forward by subject-object nonduality. This aversion to nondual models of analysis and interpretation is only now beginning to yield slightly in the face of contemporary developments arising from quantum physics and consciousness studies by such thinkers as Goswami (1993), Squires (1990, 1994), Kafatos and Nadeau (1990), Mindell (2000), Stapp (1993), and Davis (1983). An enormous adjustment then has to be made to our ontological and epistemological views as they pertain to Critical Theory and Cultural Studies. It is forcing us to radically re-evaluate our conceptions on identity and the nature of subjectivity.

The aggregate of subject-object nondualist theory, both eastern and western, remains excluded from the canon of critical theorists notwithstanding the fact that some theorists, such as the deconstructionists (e.g., Derrida), relied heavily upon a few of its principles. The need to include subject-object nondual theory within the canon has never been greater and promises nothing less than a revolution in thinking.

With this in mind, I would like to explore the nature of language and language development through the perspective of subject-object nonduality as it relates to our ideas of 'self' and 'identity'. More specifically, the Buddhist doctrine of *Anātman* ('no-self') posits that the experience of subject-object duality is, in fact, an illusion and that the fundamental nature of the individual is that it is not separate, but one, with the world. Given this fundamental proposition, language can be seen as both a primary method for asserting our individuality and separateness in the world as well as the principle bridging mechanism between that misconceived illusory identity and what is mistakenly perceived of as "the other." It is through this understanding of language that we might apprehend the power that language has to alter the way we experience reality and reconsider how we might modify language in order to transform our growth, expression and understanding of ourselves.

The Buddhist Doctrine of *Anātman*

According to the Buddhist doctrine of *Anātman*, all creation exists as a manifestation of one underlying *Attributeless Mind* or *Buddha-nature*. This all-encompassing Mind is not only responsible for the emerging appearances of the world but, in fact, *is* those appearances as they are created by the limited sensory perceptions of the senses and human brain. A reflection of itself arises in the human brain in the form of an ego or self-identity. In this way, *Attributeless Mind* seeks to express and, thereby, to know itself. It no longer experiences itself as the Absolute but instead comes to identify itself through the many individualised 'loci of awareness' in creation – the separate human mind. The individualised human egos, which are simply temporary microcosmic reflections of this whole, seek a sense of permanence for themselves and attempt to define themselves within the framework of their own limited sensory experience of the world. It is this reflexive activity of consciousness looking out in the world to identify its existence which creates the experience of separation and alienation from its own inner being. The ego becomes afflicted with a type of uneasiness and lack of fulfillment in life which the Buddhists describe as *duhkha*. This uneasiness often translates within the human being as the need to affirm or ratify a permanent sense of 'self' in the world and, if possible, in one's relationship to nature and to "God." The desire for wholeness arises inwardly and, often, unconsciously but is typically directed outwards to the form world to find wholeness – thus, unintentionally increasing the distance between the real inner self and the outer illusory self.

Unfortunately, wholeness can never be achieved in this way because the personal ego and its encasing 'identity' is, itself, not real or permanent. In Buddhist practice wholeness is achieved through embracing impermanence and renouncing (or 'detaching' from) the separative personal ego. In doing so, reality-as-it-is slowly begins to emerge into the consciousness along with the realisation that one is not the individual illusory ego-self but that there is only the Absolute *Attributeless Mind*. The practitioner comes to see that their own nature *is* this *Attributeless Mind*. As suggested in the Upaniṣadic text, "when a man sees all beings within his very self, and his self within all beings"[2] then the separation between the individual and nature will not only diminish but will be seen to have been an illusion in the first place. Man is not *in* nature, Man *is* nature. Achieving this nondual experience is said to be a long and arduous process, and eventually necessitates the entire renunciation of the subject-object ego-identity. This is not something

---

[2] *Upaniṣads*. translated by Patrick Olivelle. (New York: Oxford University Press, 1996), 249.

that is easily achieved, even where the individual is highly motivated to do so. In the interim, between being fully identified with the illusory self and the renunciation of that illusory dualistic identity, there exists a largely unconscious urge to communicate and re-establish a connection with what is only experienced as "the other" outside of oneself. In the typical person this urge sustains the need to communicate as long as one believes (consciously or unconsciously) in the possibility that some union could occur at some level with the other. Where there is the belief that no union is possible, or where one is not confident with one's own sense of identity or being-in-the-world, the desire to communicate can diminish. In this way we can see that a foundation for language can arise out of the struggle to both differentiate oneself from others and, once accomplished, to re-unite with "the other." These conflicting drives create suffering for the individual and the outer materialisation of this inner war is through projection and language.

The Dualistic Consequences of Language

Nothing so powerfully reinforces our dualistic interpretation of the world, apart from our limited sensory experience of it, as the use of language. In fact, the underlying assumption within language is that the world is based in subject-object dualism and that language bridges between two or more *distinct* identities or objects. *Our entire experience of the world is mediated in one form or another – whether that mediation be in the form of sensory perceptions, thoughts, or language.* In language we find a method for sharing part of our experiences with others. "I see the dog" is a basic expression, from me *to you*, of the belief of myself as a subject ("I") witnessing ("I see") an object ("the dog"), which is also understood as distinct from myself. The most obvious achievement of language is that it not only transmits superficial information between two parties about experience in the world (i.e., "me seeing the dog") but it also subliminally conveys and reinforces the notion that the world is filled with subjects and objects. It is declaring and reinforcing an underlying dualistic worldview that the universe is made up of separate subjects and objects. Language is, by extension, an attempt to create bridges between myself (the subject) and all of those various objects of the world experienced as "the other." This activity of sharing experience, while not itself conclusive, hints at an innate will to cooperate and unite with that "other."

This is an important point that deserves some further attention. The ramifications of the use of language, in light of what I have just stated, may illustrate that human beings have an innate urge to share and unite with "the other." If that were not true, then there is very little reason to communicate linguistically or to develop sophisticated language forms. While we might be able to advance that there are some limited expressions substantial enough to justify the continued use of language, there seems to be little compelling reason – other than the intuitive need to 'belong' or to 'cooperate' – why we should have developed such sophisticated and complex systems of language. If competitiveness is intrinsic to our nature, as some evolutionary and social theorists have maintained, then there would have been very little reason to develop widespread language sophistication in the first place. Theorists who approach this question from the bias of subject-object dualism often fail to appreciate or acknowledge the possibility that an underlying nondual nature within the human being exists as the driver behind language development and complexity. That is, we experience separateness from one another against the sensed backdrop of some subtle unity, and this leads to the advancement of a drive or impulsive reaction to bridge the experienced gap between ourselves and the objects of our environment. Humans have gone to enormous lengths to connect every far region of the planet with all other parts and yet there remain those who evidence surprise at the assertion that we are innately communicative and seek inter-connectivity as a potential outer expression of our *fundamentally unified* inner nature.

To go even deeper requires that we recognise that language is inexorably connected to thought. In fact, language is said to be the concretization of thought; it is the manifestation onto the physical plane of thoughts which arise in our minds.

Saussure wrote that our thoughts would have little meaning or form without language:

> Psychologically our thought – apart from its expression in words – is only a shapeless and indistinct mass. Philosophers and linguists have always agreed in recognising that without the help of signs we would be unable to make a clearcut, consistent distinction between two ideas. Without language, thought is a vague, uncharted nebula. There are no pre-existing ideas, and

nothing is distinct before the appearance of language.³

A nondualist would only partly endorse this position. What is implied in Saussure's assertion is that we need to define and name the thoughts that appear in our minds in order to better objectify them and to understand our subjective relation to those objects of thought. In naming and objectifying these thoughts-of-things we are then able to better "subjectify" ourselves. In terms of the Buddhist doctrine of *Anātman*, if I can determine a *that* – regardless of how illusory it may be – then I will be able to substantiate a *this* (e.g., an "I"). Our search for permanence demands that we somehow define ourselves in relation to a universe experienced as separate from us. For the individual who experiences the world dualistically (and that essentially refers to all of us in our typical sensory experience of the world), we see a tree and assign it the signification "tree" so that an incidence of "I" is distinctly affirmed as being *in relation to* that tree. However, the nondualist understands that to label or "significate" the tree would be to generate an illusion about one's relationship to the tree since the 'truth of it' is that "I am the tree and the tree is me." It is obviously a *distinct* object from me in the physical world but both 'I' and the 'tree' are also simply co-extensions of the same underlying Whole. It would not be a 'shapeless and indistinct mass', as Saussre would contend, but would be an extension of

---

³ Ferdinand de Saussure, "Course in General Linguistics" *Critical Theory Since 1965.* Edited by Hazard Adams and Leroy Searle. (Gainesville: University Presses of Florida, 1986), 649.

oneself. What is absent from the nondualist's experience compared to Saussure's 'nameless thoughts' is the *additional* belief in one's own mind of oneself as a distinct and separate existence. The nondualist perspective would refrain from holding the dualist worldview that they were separate from all that is experienced and that, as a result of this abstention, the object appearing in the mind of the nondualist (i.e. the tree) would not be *categorized* as "other" in the first place. The process of distinguishing and categorizing one's own identity as distinct does not arise. The visual perception is the same between the nondualist and the dualist thinker, but the interpretation and mental response to that perception would proceed to vastly different outcomes. In a nondualistic state of awareness, form and meaning arise within and through the essence of the moment itself rather than being imposed upon by the structure of a thoughtform which is being created by the dualistic perceiver. The dualist observer is literally seeing the world as if through a set of 'idea filters' (belief systems) which render its interpretation of the world in terms of subject-object relationships. According to the doctrine of 'no-self,' our need to communicate and develop tools for that communication (i.e., language) can only occur if one has *already* psychologically separated oneself from the world. Likewise, as one retraces their steps and begins to dissolve the identity of being a separate ego, language becomes increasingly inadequate and paradoxical when relating with the world of outer form – for how can one speak of the formless world using tools (language) designed to describe the world in terms of separate forms.

Émile Benveniste took a more philosophical approach to linguistics than Saussure. In examining more closely the actual source of language, he reversed Saussure's view by linking the creation of subjectivity in the individual to the use of the term "I" in language.

> It is in and through language that man constitutes himself as a *subject*, because language alone establishes the concept of 'ego' in reality, in *its* reality which is that of being...
> Consciousness of self is only possible if it is experienced by contrast. I use *I* only when I am speaking to someone who will be a *you* in my address...
> This polarity of persons is the fundamental condition in language, of which the process of communication, in which we share, is only a mere pragmatic consequence.[4]

The assertion is that subjectivity *arises out of the use of language*. That is, language becomes the creative agent of subjectivity "so that it is literally true that the basis of subjectivity is in the exercise of language. If one really thinks about it, one will see that there is no other objective testimony to the identity of the subject except that which he himself thus gives about himself."[5] This statement supports the notion that language produces subjectivity. His statement describes a subjectivity whose existence and further reinforcement is actually *created* by the use of language. The Buddhist

---

[4] Émile Benveniste, "Subjectivity in Language" *Critical Theory Since 1965*. Edited by Hazard Adams and Leroy Searle. (Gainesville: University Presses of Florida, 1986), 729.
[5] Benveniste, 730.

doctrine of *Anātman* appears to hold true in that the underlying *Attributeless Mind* identifies itself with the particular 'loci of awareness' and, in that state of individuated and fragmented experience, seeks to substantiate its limited illusory existence through the use of language. This fragmented perspective, which is the personal ego, establishes a sense of lack or disconnection in the individual who then seeks to re-establish his innate unified nature and relationship to all things by utilizing language as the bridging mechanism with what is perceived as other subjects. This sense of disconnection generates the internal conflict and uneasiness – known in Eastern traditions as *duhkha* – which Buddhism illustrates as one of the central characteristics of human existence. Language is used as both the tool to acknowledge one's individual existence as well as the means to overcome that outer separation and re-establish a unifying bridge with other individuals. Later, language becomes a tool for understanding as the search turns inward, and the needs for language in oneself is eventually transcended altogether once a full inner unity is established (i.e., enlightened or liberated state). Language is then no longer a bridging tool, but serves as a medium of contact and instruction with those who are still as yet to transcend the fragmented and separate state of identity.

An interesting feature of the spoken word is that it seems to carry the power to unfurl thoughts into physical forms. Language is a bridge – a *coping mechanism* if you will – between the individual and the world that they experience as separate from themselves; it is a tool for individuals who have no internal way to relate to a fragmented world within which they have come to believe they exist. By internal I mean that, because our experience is dominated by our sensory perspective of the world, there is no direct *inner* experience of nonduality or oneness within the individual's present sphere of experience. Language is personally no longer necessary where the individual has achieved *complete* fusion or *interconnectivity* with the Whole within which they previously appeared to exist. It is only under the perceptual framework of dualism – where reality is psychologically projected and registered as existing separate from oneself – that a need to connect with others arises and compels the development of language to bridge those barriers.

This speaks to what appears to be an *a priori* association or underlying interdependence of humanity with a universe of which they envision themselves a part. From the perspective of *Buddha-nature* one is not ontologically separate from the world but, instead, one suffers from an *epistemological* separation – that is, an outer world that only *appears* separate. What arises as an involuntary urge toward unity logically *precedes* language and acts as the stimulus to further develop communication and cooperation. Despite the contrary view presented by Hobbes that life is "solitary, poor, nasty, brutish and short," one wonders how an inherent need for the human species to communicate and propagate community could be re-interpreted by Hobbes as some fanciful 'natural disposition' within human nature that would "render men apt to invade, and destroy one another."[6] Rather, it is only in the fixation upon and championing of a separative dualistic perspective that this brutish rendition of the human species could be forwarded at all. In this alone we can see how the bias to read human nature as competitive, aggressive, or separative arises out of the analytical perspective of subject-object dualism.

Regardless of how fractured 17th century Europe may have appeared to Hobbes, the historical accounts of civilisation do not necessarily bear witness to his assertions when viewed through the panorama of nonduality. Despite the destruction and devastation suffered by humanity over the ages, one would think that we would have by now acquired a permanent and irreversible aversion to one another. Notwithstanding the growing pains that we have observed in humanity's development, the march toward establishing larger associations and fellowships continues to this day – so much so, that our evolutionary advancement demands that we achieve political, economic and cultural unity on a global scale. Yet, it has been our ill-conceived ontological belief in the notions of separateness which have, at times, thwarted our best efforts to unity and cooperation, and fragmented human society. Regardless, no matter how devastating humans have been to one another, there remains the recurring drive toward unification and cooperation. The continued development and use of language is specifically demonstrative of this essential drive to unity.

---

[6] Thomas Hobbes, *Leviathan*. (Cambridge: Cambridge University Press, 1997), 89.

It would seem obvious to us that the best mechanism for survival is cooperation and language appears as a pre-eminent example of the attempt to rise above the circumstances of separation, although the fears which produce division are often hard to overcome. Competition is touted as the *modus operandi* for many supporters of the current western free market economic model. The method of interaction is simply too "expensive," in psychological and emotional terms, to maintain in the long run and requires massive amounts of energy to sustain what are temporary illusions of security.

It is obvious that complex language is less and less necessary as the level of competition is increased. At a point of absolute competition between individuals, little language, if any, is required. One would simply need to ward off competitors through individual strategies. Even those who wish to cooperate to fulfill common competitive ends must eventually compete against one another. The degree of sophistication presently found in language (i.e., poetry, philosophy, music, art, science, religion, etc) suggests a more substantial push toward unity within the human family in spite of the alienation engendered through some systems of social and economic competition today. It hardly seems worth the energy that has been expended throughout the vast history of human civilisation, developing so many complex means of communication across such a wide expanse of socio-economic models, only to accommodate what evolutionary biologists would describe as a mass competitive strategy for survival. We have continued to develop language as a means of bridging the *apparent* gulf between ourselves and others. This is significant and cannot be ignored.

The Inadequacy of Language to Describe Nonduality

The existence of language, as a result of dualistic experience, raises further issues for us. Not only does it mirror to us the way we perceive the world, it also *reinforces* that view. Every sentence we utter has the additional effect of crystallising our perspective and belief systems. This occurs so much that it strengthens our base assumptions about the universe as dual in nature. In order to adopt language as a bridging tool with others we actually create and reinforce a further distinction in our minds between ourselves and others. What is originally intended as a unifying activity turns out to be a two edged sword and maintains a perspective that subtly continues to alienate us from the rest of the world.

In order to ultimately bridge the gap we need to transcend the use of language – or, perhaps, develop a new form of language. Within the doctrine of *Anātman* it would mean recognising the illusory nature of the personal ego and renouncing that ego as the locus of identity and awareness. In such an event, a society would need to acknowledge the fundamental unity behind life and then *consciously* build unity into the social framework. From this, a language of nonduality would naturally arise.

An unconscious sense of this unity is now being evidenced in many areas of social life. It is achieved through a slow but steady process of thought and thought-form deconstruction which we have previously come to accept as the traditional views of reality. Until now, language has provided a mental framework for us to articulate the world around us; it is also a framework which comes to reflexively affect the way we see ourselves in the world. This is not the true nondual nature of the reality but only our perspective of reality through the limited sensory input of our experience. As David Loy suggests, what is constructed can also be deconstructed. Loy expands further on this point:

> The nondualist agrees that such dualities [e.g., identity/non-identity] are ineluctably inscribed in language and thus are fundamental categories of thought; however, this means not that they are inescapable, but that their deconstruction points finally to an experience beyond language – or, more precisely, to a nondual way of experiencing language and thought.[7]

The move to globalisation in a social sense will inevitably lead to a need to understand the world nondually and to find ways to communicate nondually. A starting point is in seeing that the language we use to describe the world around us is a limitation that prevents us from moving to a true nondualist interaction with others, with nature, and with the universe around us. Humanity has evidenced profound leaps in discovery where necessity has demanded it. At this point, the recognition of nondualism as constituting the next paradigm or level of understanding for humanity could incite a

---

[7] David Loy, *Nonduality: A Study of Comparative Philosophy*. (New York: Humanity Books, 1998), 250.

movement toward such knowledge that is unrivalled in history.

> Unarticulated and delusive ontological commitments underlie even the most everyday uses of language. Suddenly, language/thought is no longer the means (as according to metaphysics), nor even the end (according to Heidegger and Derrida, in very different ways), *but the problem itself* [emphasis mine]. Philosophy cannot grasp what it seeks in any of its categories, but, as language becoming self-conscious of its function, it can learn to 'undo' itself and cease to be an obstruction, in that way allowing what we have long sought to manifest itself. This 'origin-that-cannot-be-named' has always been the most obvious thing, but all ways of thinking about it – whether metaphysical or deconstructive – can only conceal it by dualistically separating us from it.[8]

The inadequacy of language to properly describe nonduality accounts for many paradoxes found within the Buddhist teachings. Situated throughout the many teachings attributed to the Buddha are phrases that speak of achievement in relinquishing goals, or of 'attaining life by renouncing life'.

> When a man considers this world as a bubble of froth, and as the illusion of an appearance, then the king of death has no power over him...
> Better than power over all the earth, better than going to heaven and better than dominion over the worlds is the joy of the man who enters the river of life that leads to *nirvāṇa*.[9]

---

[8] Loy, 250-51.
[9] *The Dhammapada*. Translated by Juan Mascaró. (London: Penguin Books, 1973), 60-61.

The limitations of language are clearly implied in this example of the Buddha's metaphor for traveling the correct path to awakening. What is being taught is that *nirvāṇa* requires a shift of *perspective*. Yet, language is inadequate to describe exactly what is *nirvāṇa*. Where, indeed, is *nirvāṇa*? The question is misleading because *nirvāṇa* is right here in every moment of our existence. Our inability to "recognise" it demonstrates the power of dualistic thinking to impose itself on our epistemological interpretation of the world. Despite the insufficiency of the language above to give us a clear material direction to follow, *nirvāṇa* requires a mere epistemological shift in our awareness of the world. Language hardly seems adequate to deal with the task at hand yet hints that our nature is beyond all language and thought-naming activities. From the perspective of our limited sensory awareness, however, language is the tool *par excellence* for uniting us with others and bringing our development nearer to achieving *nirvāṇa*. The final step requires a release from language altogether as it can serve no other purpose than to continue reaffirming a dualistic frame of mind.

Our discussion to this point should be sufficient to impress upon the mind of the reader that language imposes a great deal upon our interpretation of reality. It should be clear by now that all of our experiences are mediated in some form, whether through the sense apparatus or via language. It is true to say that language is itself a metaphor for reality used to classify and communicate a belief about ourselves as subjects located in time and space. We create the categories in language to describe the experience we have of a world that is perceived to be outside of us and which, due to the nature of sensual experience, is dualistic in appearance. This epistemological short-sightedness drastically undermines our approach to both science and critical theory and, if left unchecked, eventually results in a shift toward 'scientism' that is dangerous and narrow-minded in its perspective.

Habermas described scientism this way: "'Scientism' means science's belief in itself: that is, the conviction that we can no longer understand science as one form of possible knowledge, but rather must identify knowledge with science."[10] This mis-identification of knowledge with science served as a springboard to co-opt the traditions of empiricism and rationalism to "strengthen science's belief in its exclusive validity."[11] This move was instrumental in the early assertion of the dominion of science over other forms of inquiry in the 19th and 20th centuries. In turn, this led to an abatement of reflection upon the nature of knowledge, as evidenced by such thinkers as Hume or Kant, and curtailed epistemological investigation. In some important ways, we have come to stop asking how we develop knowledge about ourselves and the world around us. In its place we grant science the given that it will automatically provide correct knowledge. This is a hazardous position to hold where science is concerned because it leads to a centralisation and calcification of worldviews. Science, having

---

[10] Jürgen Habermas, *Knowledge and Human Interests*. (Boston: Beacon Press, 1968), 4.
[11] Habermas, 4.

established its own unassailable metaphysical parameters is then forced to live within those boundaries and maintain the illusion that it is making progress. In fact, the opposite occurs and few minds are supported who think outside of the current (dualist) ontological framework; a danger which has been evident in the fields of Critical Theory and Cultural Studies. This is what led Habermas to the claim that we require a non-scientific methodology when dealing with the social sciences.[12] It is a good case to make in respect to studies across all areas of Humanities. The danger of surrendering to an empirical dualistic viewpoint has obviously passed into the canon of Critical Theory and will, in time, render the canon illegitimate and obsolete if it is unable to accept nondualist theory.

As an example of the danger we have identified, some writers in Critical Theory have attempted to make the claim that consciousness, as a feature of the human being, is exclusively a biological feature of the material brain (Dennett, 1995) (Searle, 1992, 1995, 1998). That is, the assertion suggests that because an individual is conscious, and that that consciousness is identified within the brain, then that brain must be the source of consciousness. Here we have an example of the notion previously described by Whitehead as arriving to conclusions through the *method of difference*:

> The difficulty has its seat in the empirical side of philosophy. Our datum is the actual world, including ourselves; and this actual world spreads itself for observation in the guise of the

---

[12] William Outwaite, *Habermas: A Critical Introduction*. (Stanford: Stanford University Press, 1994), 26.

topic of our immediate experience. The elucidation of immediate experience is the sole justification for any thought; and the starting-point for thought is the analytic observation of components of this experience. But we are not conscious of any clear-cut complete analysis of immediate experience, in terms of the various details which comprise its definiteness. We habitually observe by the method of difference. Sometimes we see an elephant, and sometimes we do not. The result is that an elephant, when present, is noticed. Facility of observation depends on the fact that the object observed is important when present, and sometimes is absent.[13]

As I suggested earlier, we depend upon our observations of the world as the beginning and the end for analysing experience. Given that, we are already biased toward subject-object homogeneity and, because our sensory experience presents us with a dualistic picture of the world, find it hard to avoid dualist assumptions about all of reality. This *method of difference*, as Whitehead describes it, leaves us at the same point that we began in merely having traversed the same ground of "empirical" (observable) evidence in order to substantiate our initial ego-centric dualist bias. It is as though we are caught in a conceptual feed-back loop, unable to break free of dualist assertions because of our self-assurance in the ongoing appraisals of sensory input. What this amounts to is a relatively unconscious formulaic approach to all endeavours of our experience (including academic investigation) which assert that

---

[13] Alfred North Whitehead, *Process and Reality.* Corrected Edition (New York: The Free Press, 1978),4.

appearance is somehow equivalent to reality. The 'rational' leap regarding consciousness for those operating from within a dualistic perspective is made by asserting that the mere appearance of consciousness in the human body necessitates that consciousness was somehow *created* by the result of bodily activity. The confidence evinced by some who hold this position is reflected in the words of John R. Searle, Professor of Philosophy at the University of California at Berkeley: "We know for a fact that all of our conscious states are caused by brain processes...one thing that we have to accept before we ever get going in this discussion is that, in fact, brain processes do cause consciousness."[14] By all accounts this assertion is completely unfounded. There are simply no grounds for which to make such a statement. From this unproven position, he is then able to put forth his further notions and, in effect, make a category mistake in the process. This follows entirely from the reason that he is locked within a dualist perspective on the subject:

> I do not think that we are forced to either dualism or materialism. The point to remember is that consciousness is a biological phenomenon like any other. It is true that it has special features, most notably the feature of subjectivity, but that does not prevent consciousness from being a higher-level feature of the brain in the same way that digestion is a higher-level feature of the stomach, or liquidity a higher-level feature of the system of molecules that constitute our blood. In short, the way to reply to materialism is to point

---

[14] John R. Searle, *Mind, Language, and Society*. (New York: Basic Books, 1998), 51.

out that it ignores the real existence of consciousness. The way to defeat dualism is simply to refuse to accept the categories that make consciousness out as something non-biological, not a part of the natural world.[15]

Searle is trying to provide a solution to the mind/body problem in his references to overcoming the position of dualism. However, he is visibly stuck 'in the box' of dualist thinking in his dependence upon the (biological) appearances of the world as necessarily providing the only possible source for consciousness. To compare consciousness, as he does, to digestion as a higher-level feature of the stomach or to liquidity as a higher-level feature of the system of molecules that constitute our blood, is simply to say that consciousness is a quality or predicate of the physical brain. His argument appears to be consistent until one recognises that he has made a category mistake in equating consciousness with other categories of which one is *conscious of in the first place* (i.e. digestion, liquidity). To follow this line of reasoning, consciousness would need to be conscious of itself directly from a second 'higher level' rather than simply through the reflection of its *effects in the world*, as is currently the case. Despite the fact that this is simply bad logic, it does nothing to further our understanding of language. Searle wishes to first ground the subject-object dualistic notion of 'self' arising in a biological process and then, like Lacan, attribute the structure of language to the structure of the unconscious.[16]

---

[15] Searle, 51-2.
[16] Jacques Lacan, "The Agency of the Letter in the Unconscious or Reason Since Freud." *Critical Theory*

What is not questioned by either author is whether the "I" is an actual self-existing being in the first place. If language is dependent upon the structure of the unconscious mind, then one could suppose that language could arise even where a personal identity is not constructed in the conscious mind. The contradictions are obvious wherein, without the creation of an "I", there is no *intention* for the expression of language. Instead, it is the creation of an identity – an "I" – which precedes both the intention to communicate (from this locus of individuality to another) as well as the structure of that language (from the perspective of an "I") within the unconscious.

Searle's general approach to the problem assumes that our immediate experience of the world, within the parameters of subject-object duality, can bear witness to an ontological or actual inference about reality. That is, we can see his efforts as a struggle to posit an explanation for conscious experience while taking for granted that his subject-object experience is, in some way, an accurate portrayal of reality-as-it-is. This is a clear example of Whitehead's elucidation on the method of difference employed by dualist empiricists and we can witness the subject-object dualist's error in assuming that *appearance* equals *reality*.

For Searle, this appearance constitutes the limit of consciousness – as a higher-level function of the biological brain – and language is therefore the *modus operandi* that consciousness

---

Since 1965. Edited by Hazard Adams and Leroy Searle. (Gainesville: University Presses of Florida, 1986), 738-53.

implements in order to create the individuality which is a language-being. Intentionality is an important part of communication and, for the most part, intentionality is *integral* to the act of communication. Searle describes intentionality as "that feature of the mind by which mental states are directed at, or are about or of, or refer to, or aim at, states of affairs in the world."[17] Here we see that Searle understands 'intention' as a feature solely connected to the world, or experiences of the world, and of a consciousness that functions within the boundaries of the subject-object paradigm. He might say, in fact, that intentionality exists *only* within the sphere of subject-object experiences, where one's belief of the world is projected outside of oneself. Within nondual experience, where one identifies with the event as a whole, there can be no intention toward or about 'things.' There is no *personal* intention toward another, like there is no need for language and communication, because one is both subject and object or, more accurately, one is neither subject nor object. There is no one else, distinct from oneself, to communicate *to*. Of course, our current dualistic experience of the world is still rooted in the subject-object framework. Therefore, language remains necessary. However, our goal here was to examine the source of language through a perspective of nondualism; a perspective which is normally unconscious within the individual yet drives behaviour toward unity and connectivity (communication).

Finally, Searle fails to provide for any notion of identity consciousness that could account for

---

[17] Searle, 64-5.

a nondual or non-linear experience, such as Jung's investigations on *synchronicity*. However, it is premature to write off Searle's position entirely without offering the possibility of an alternative. That is to say, is it possible to employ language in a way that helps us move beyond the method of difference and closer to a nondualistic perception of the world?

Can We Learn to Communicate Nondually?

We are discovering the need to begin moving beyond the limitations that dualistic systems of language impose. This is not entirely new in the history of human development and some cultures have attempted to incorporate this notion of a nondual identity into their language. One such example of the use of language to 'offset' some of the dualist tendencies of our experience can be found within the Tibetan language. Considered to belong to its own distinct language group, Tibetan is interesting in that it belongs to a less common class of languages consisting of what is termed *ergative*.[18] In ergative languages, a unique style

---

[18] Other *ergative* languages include Basque, some Caucasus languages like Georgian and Chechen, the early but now extinct Mesopetamian languages like Hurrian and Sumerian, Chinook, Panoan languages (Peru, Brazil, Bolivia), Mayan, most Australian Aboriginal languages and Eskimo-Aleut languages. It is interesting to note that ergative languages are particular to certain regions of the world and are often the foundation of either 'pre-modern civilisation' languages or native and indigenous peoples' languages. One wonders whether the advance of civilisation and development of a more ego-centric

arises where the subject of a transitive verb behaves like the object of a transitive verb. This is in contrast to English which is *nominative-accusative*, and where the subject of a transitive verb behaves like the agent of that transitive verb. Essentially, the main subject in an English sentence becomes viewed in Tibetan as an object within the unfolding event or activity. This has the curious effect of rendering the typical nominative-accusative subject into thematic subject. Focus on a central actor performing an action changes to a focus on the unfolding theme within which an actor is participating. While this may seem inconsequential at first glance, it is this shifting emphasis away from a central nominative-accusative role which reorients how the Tibetan interprets their experience of events.

Tibetan culture is grounded in Buddhist principles and so it should not be seen as unusual that the Tibetan language would employ the use of thematic events as a central organising grammatical principle rather than focusing on a specific individual as the subject of reference. This serves to reinforce the Buddhist belief that the subject – the "I" – is an illusion and not central (or even essential) to their experience. For example, let us suppose that I am hauling water from a distant well to my house. My English description of the incident would start with a declaration of intent on my part as the central subject of the activity: "I am carrying water up the hill." The Tibetan speaker, when relating their account of events in their native tongue, would adjust the emphasis of

---

mental perspective has been a factor in the diminishment of the ergative structure in language.

perspective in the event so that the 'I' is no longer the central subject: "The water is being carried (by me)." In this case, the 'carrying of the water' is now the main theme of the experience and the fact that it was being 'done by me' is only incidental and implied to the unfolding event.

This use of language reflects the emphasis on the *Anātman* doctrine of 'no-self' within Tibetan Buddhist culture. The essential sensory experience of a subject-object reality still exists for Tibetans. However, a shift of emphasis within the language diminishes (although not entirely eliminates) the sense of self- or ego-importance in the individual and this influence pervades all interactions within Tibetan culture.[19] Their personal interpretations of experience become, to some degree, de-centralised along with their own sense of identity. When utilised efficiently, language can substantially alter our perception of the role we have in relation to the universe.

In his article on "The Relation of Habitual Thought and Behavior to Language," Benjamin Lee Whorf lays the groundwork of his notions on language by providing a quote from Edward Sapir:

> The fact of the matter is that the 'real world' is to a large extent unconsciously built upon the language habits of the group.... We see and hear and otherwise experience very largely, as we do

---

[19] I do not wish to give the impression that Tibetans are typically ego-less or free of any mark of self-centeredness due to their use of language. Rather, I wish to show how the use of language can be, and has been, used as an influential tool for manipulating one's experience and relation to reality.

because the language habits of our community predispose certain choices of interpretation."[20]

Whorf demonstrates this notion by illustrating how *language* arranges the data we receive to fit our pre-formed conception of the world. In comparing the Hopi language to what he defines as the Standard Average European of language (SAE), Whorf found that notions of time, space, and matter were understood in radically different ways relative to how members in each culture viewed themselves in relation the world. The Hopi experienced the world through a nondual worldview and this dramatically altered their expression of language. Where European culture saw itself subject to the influences of time, space, and matter, the Hopi saw themselves as undifferentiated in any way from time, space, and matter. Where Europeans described the individual as existing *in* linear time the Hopi could only describe reality in terms of the ever present *now*. Finally, where the west viewed individuals located *in* space, as though they were somehow separate from it, the Hopi expressed a form of nondualist thought which identified them *as* the expression of space itself. As Whorf explains,

> Monistic, holistic, and relativistic views of reality appeal to philosophers and some scientists, but they are badly handicapped in appealing to the 'common sense' of the western average man – not because nature herself refutes them (if she did,

---

[20] Benjamin Whorf, "The Relation of Habitual Thought and Behavior to Language." *Critical Theory Since 1965*. Edited by Hazard Adams and Leroy Searle. (Gainesville: University Presses of Florida, 1986), 710.

philosophers could have discovered this much), but because they must be talked about in what amounts to a new language.[21]

This new language for holistic or nondual experience is illustrated somewhat in both the Hopi and Tibetan cultures and shows that language reflects one's view of the 'self' in that world, rather than existing as an innate structure within the unconscious mind. As Whorf concedes,

> Science is beginning to find that there is something in the cosmos that is not in accord with the concepts we have formed in mounting the spiral [of dualist thinking]. It is trying to frame a *new language* by which to adjust itself to a wider universe.[22]

This idea of changing our mental perspective by changing our use of language is an interesting one worth considering further in relation to subject-object nondualism. Some linguists have come to recognise the power of language as producing enormous changes in the consciousness of the individual who undergoes linguistic training (or re-training). Despite this, many continue to hold to the dogmatic anthropocentric perspective that it is impossible for linguistic beings to communicate coherently about objects in their environment without possessing a formal concept of 'Self' or 'Self-identity.' In his book, *Self-Knowledge and Social Relations*, John King-Farlow, Professor Emeritus at the University of Alberta, undercut this notion

---

[21] Whorf, 720.
[22] Whorf, 720-21.

by providing an example of such a possibility in his *Parable of the Whispering Trees*.[23] He demonstrated that it is not only possible to imagine linguistic beings able to communicate without a formal concept of 'I' but that it is also possible to construct a language capable of expressing, to some extent, the experience of subject-object nondualism. Viewing the world of 'appearances' and 'forms' as simple attributes or predicates of the all-pervading underlying 'One' (e.g., as also is *Buddha-nature* in Buddhism or *Brahman* in Advaita Vedanta), King-Farlow offers the linguistic paradigm of "IT-ish" as a language-vehicle to accommodate language-beings who hold the subject-object nondualist perspective.[24] Imagine for a moment that the universe is in fact one *Being*; thought of, perhaps, in terms of the Hindu *Brahman* or F. H. Bradley's *Absolute*. We can ascribe to this underlying Being the designation of 'IT.' The experiences which we normally encounter through a dualist perspective can now be reinterpreted in terms of a nondualist experience. That is, we no longer witness the appearance of autonomous independent entities in action but, rather, describe these 'entities' as simple attributes, manifestations, or descriptors of IT. Therefore, our expressions of events merely become *instances* of IT. A few examples may serve to provide a clearer picture of this perspective. Let us use a subject named John.

---

[23] John King-Farlow, *Self-Knowledge and Social Relations*. (New York: Science History Publications, 1978), 84-96.
[24] King-Farlow, 108-114.

> English: "I am happy."
> IT-ish: "IT John-like is happy-wise."

In the language of IT-ish we witness a shift in the main subject from the "I" (i.e., John), representing the separate individual in the English version, to the "IT" which represents all of reality. The individual "I" becomes a simple attribute (the attribute of "John-ness") of the all-encompassing "IT". The same is true in the following:

> English: "What shall I eat today?"
>
> IT-ish: "IT eats. What does IT John-like eat-wise when IT todays?"

And, likewise, in this third instance of IT-ish:

> English: "Come here and let's play."
>
> IT-ish: "Let IT be here-ed and let IT play-play."

With some practice, anyone can develop this language, or something similar to it, to effect real changes in the way that they interpret the world – linguistically and, eventually, experientially. The key feature here is that the identity of the individual as a separate entity (i.e. John) now sees itself as some aspect of "IT", and so becomes conceptually altered in their sense of inner identity or idea of themselves. The experience is still subjective, but the interpretation of that subjectivity is that its existence is as an aspect of the collective rather than as an autonomous or separate being unto itself. In time, if one can condition one's thinking to automatically adopt this view, in the same way that we are presently conditioned to communicate in dualist terms and from a disconnected and separative view, it is likely that everything having to do with our interaction in the world will take on a dramatically new flavour. I think that one important thing to notice here is that the empirical experience of the world does not necessarily need to change – only our mental interpretation of that experience. As Nāgārjuna suggested, the dual and the nondual world are the same. It is only our interpretation that changes. "There is no difference at all between Samsāra and Nirvāṇa."[25]

This is a demonstration of linguistic 'interference' and accounts for many of the contradictions and paradoxes that we find when approaching descriptions of a nondual reality. Language is inadequate, as it now exists, to articulate reality in terms of a nondual metaphysic. This was clearly understood by the Buddha as the highest form of knowledge and was exemplified often by his demonstrations of silence.

Language as a Bridging Mechanism

The notion of personal *intentionality* is clearly a feature that arises only within the dualist experience of reality. Clearly, where one has a nondual experience of reality, there can be no intention toward anything because one *is* everything; at least that is what one is experiencing. This absence of 'lack' leaves the individual free to act according to the conditions

---

[25] Stcherbatsky, Theodore. *The Conception of Buddhist Nirvāṇa*. (New York: Gordon Press, 1973), 117.

of the moment without an imposition upon their experience or re-interpretation of reality by the ego. Habermas takes the idea of intentionality into account and develops his argument by looking at the human species as a group impelled toward unity:

> ...society is not only a system of self-preservation. An enticing natural force, present in the individual as libido, has detached itself from the behavioral system of self-preservation and urges toward utopian fulfillment...What may appear as naked survival...is subject to the criterion of what a society intends for itself as *the good life*.[26]

Habermas recognises that the human species steps beyond the definition of being a mere animal in nature. While we maintain the instinctual drive to self-preservation, we harness that impulse within what appears to be a greater understanding or gravitation toward social unity and harmony. From this position he further posits the search for knowledge as intrinsic to human growth. Within that thesis are three main categories of knowledge:

> The specific viewpoints from which, with transcendental necessity, we apprehend reality ground three categories of possible knowledge: information that expands our knowledge of technical control [i.e. empirical knowledge]; interpretations that make possible the orientation of action within common traditions [i.e. historical or hermeneutical knowledge]; and analyses that free consciousness from its dependence on hypostatized powers [emancipatory knowledge].[27]

---

[26] Habermas, 312-13.
[27] Habermas, 313.

Habermas provides these three types of knowledge as the categories which "establish the specific viewpoints from which we can apprehend reality as such in any way whatsoever. By becoming aware of the impossibility of getting beyond these transcendental limits, a part of nature acquires, through us, autonomy in nature."[28] It is the last of these categories, *knowledge leading to emancipation*, which brings Habermas to a critical point pertaining to our theme. It is this knowledge toward emancipation, through self-reflection, that provides for the human interest in autonomy and responsibility:

> The human interest in autonomy and responsibility is not mere fancy, for it can be apprehended a priori. What raises us out of nature is the only thing in nature that we can really know: *language*. Through its structure, autonomy and responsibility are posited for us. Our first sentence expresses unequivocally the *intention of universal and unconstrained consensus* [emphasis mine].[29]

The claim made by Habermas is that language, with all of its capacity for subtlety, is evidence for an *a priori* interest within the human species toward unity and consensus. To speak even one sentence is evidence to the universe of the 'intention of universal and unconstrained consensus.' The development and use of language is conclusive of our need for consensus and unity.

---

[28] Habermas, 311.
[29] Habermas, 314.

The question of confrontation within or between social networks arises as the objection to Habermas' claim. The response to this objection comes in understanding that the goal of unity and harmony within society can only be realised in relationship to the level of development achieved by its individual members:

> ...only in an emancipated society, whose members' autonomy and responsibility had been realised, would communication have developed into the non-authoritarian and universally practiced dialogue from which both our model of reciprocally constituted ego identity and our idea of true consensus are always implicitly derived. To this extent the truth of statements is based on anticipating the realisation of the good life.[30]

For Habermas, truth statements and truth in communication depend upon the degree to which society has come to realise its utopian externalisation of unity and universal consensus generated by the *a priori* human interest in autonomy and responsibility. Language, if I understand his position correctly, describes the externalisation of, and interest or drive toward, unity. The fact that we communicate in any meaningful way reflects an *a priori* interest toward unity (evidenced periodically as a social system). Therefore, the conditions of language become very important for reflecting back to us our reality, and the accuracy of truth statements, as we have seen, will depend upon that society's understanding relative to the three categories of knowledge. This is an important point because it brings us back to the dualist

---

[30] Habermas, 314.

influence of scientism and its monopoly over metaphysical truth. It is this rigidity within the dualistic empirical view which is presently preventing society from actualising social unity and universal consensus. According to the potentials of Habermas' theory, knowledge leading to emancipation is the key to releasing the growth potential within the human species and liberating our knowledge about reality from "seemingly natural constraint."[31] In other words, this would represent a move from dualist to nondualist conceptions and descriptions of reality.

Habermas goes on to provide a description concerning the natural 'background' consensus existing between individuals. As William Outwaite describes, Habermas has argued that, "acts of linguistic communication...pre-suppose four validity claims: that what we say is comprehensible, that it is true, that it is right, i.e. that there is a normative basis for the utterance, and that it is a sincere (*wahrhaftig*) expression of the speaker's feelings."[32] The idea behind his statements on validity claims that any communicative act contains the implicit notion that the statement could be justified if necessary leading eventually to a *consensus*. Without that, language would serve very little practical use. As Habermas suggested earlier, despite the threat that we might encounter during our use of language, the mere use of it at all "expresses unequivocally the intention of universal and unconstrained consensus."[33]

---

[31] Habermas, 311.
[32] Outwaite, 40.
[33] Habermas, 314.

Conclusion

Language, apart from the input from our sensory equipment, may be one of the most powerful conditioning agents that our minds encounter. Its use and misuse can imprison our perspectives of the world. Yet, it can also enable us to work toward fulfilling an *a priori* human need to unify and harmonise our existence within the universe. We continually develop more sophisticated forms of linguistic communication to express an ever subtler sense of ourselves. However, the nature of language remains dualistic, owing to the rigid ontological categories imposed by the empirical view of reality. The important point here is that the *categories, such as those found in language, are neither foundational nor intrinsic.* Rather, the categories are simply what we create from our perception of ourselves in the world that allows us to deal with our dualist perspective. These categories are woven into language and become the self-reinforcing mechanisms that condition our further experiences of reality and our existence within that reality.

Currently, language imposes a dualist viewpoint on our mental environment. However, that is only because we have developed language historically around an unquestioned dualistically oriented chronicle of experience. We have accepted the erroneous assumption that *appearance* is equivalent to *reality* when, in fact, logical and rational determinations discount this. Nevertheless, we persist in this problematic endeavour. As Habermas has pointed out, knowledge leading to emancipation is needed in order to release humanity from "seemingly natural constraints" and without this periodic release humanity will lose both autonomy and responsibility in the world. This loss could only lead to destruction of both us and nature. The regulation of ontological, epistemological and metaphysical knowledge via the dualist constraints of scientism (through its subjugation of empiricism and rationalism) threatens to curtail the movement of society toward realising its utopian expression of the *good life*. Those who control language, in a very real way, control the minds of the populace. What is needed is a transformation in language designed to free it from the 'seemingly natural constraints' of dualism and the subject-object dichotomy. Likewise, we might encourage a broader institutional inclusion of nondualist theory within the canon of Critical Theory and Cultural Studies. In this way, a revolution in thinking could occur surpassing that of anything in previous history.

Nonduality and Enlightenment In Tibetan Buddhist Shamanism

> Even after the Truth has been realised, there remains that strong, obstinate impression that one is still an ego – the agent and experiencer. This has to be carefully removed by living in a state of constant identification with the supreme non-dual Self. Full Awakening is the eventual ceasing of all the mental impressions of being an ego.
> —*Shankaracharya*

Necessary to the fulfillment of the shaman's vocation is the attainment of altered states of consciousness through which the shaman can affect change in the human realm. Geoffrey Samuel's *Civilized Shamans: Buddhism in Tibetan Societies*[1] characterises the role of the shaman amongst differing approaches to Buddhism within Tibetan society and he compares two aspects of Tibetan Buddhism – *Shamanic* and *Clerical* – as approaches which ultimately "share the common goal of Enlightenment."[2] His comparison revolves around the fact that both approaches utilise tantric visualisation techniques as a method of achieving altered states of consciousness. Samuel's assertion is that the altered states in shamanic practice are preparatory and conducive to the enlightened

---

[1] Geoffrey Samuel, *Civilized Shamans: Buddhism in Tibetan Societies*. (Washington: Smithsonian Institution Press, 1993).
[2] Samuel, 9-10.

state (Nirvana). I intend to show, however, that Samuel is incorrect in maintaining this association and that he has committed a *category mistake* in comparing shamanic altered states with states of enlightenment – despite the fact that they both utilise tantric techniques.³ Tibetan Shamanic Buddhists operate within a dualistic point of view about the world and utilise tantric techniques to extend the limits of that view. Their aim, in effect, is to develop an expanded psychological realm of activity to gain access to a broader range of 'worlds' including the spiritual realm. The enlightened state, on the other hand, represents more than a mere adjustment in the access to 'other worlds' and is a condition of nondual awareness which exists as a result of the actual *elimination* of conceptual framework-making altogether – including any separate or distinct notion of 'self' as an actually existing subject. Here, the tantric practitioner uses tantric techniques to annihilate the experience of subject-object duality altogether through the elimination of the subjective 'self'.

From the Tibetan Clerical Buddhist's point of view, the shaman's use of tantric methods is erroneous and incomplete and only serves to extend and reinforce the practitioner's illusory experience of the world (as dualistic) into the spirit realm. The shaman, with regard to his

---

³ A *category mistake* is when a mistake arises in the attribution of the properties of a thing to the thing itself. Gilbert Ryle introduced this notion in his book *The Concept of Mind* (1949) and used the example of a visitor to Oxford, upon viewing the various buildings and library, went on to inquire, "But where is the University?" Another version of this is "not seeing the forest for the trees."

experience of the subjective world, is actually immersed in a *wider* range of illusion than is the common individual in society.

To unpack this view in more detail I will contrast the notions put forward by Samuel regarding shamanism against the nondualist notion of enlightenment found in both Madhyamaka and Yogacara Buddhist philosophy.[4] This will entail an investigation and understanding of the traditionally defined nondual condition of Nirvana itself and the recognition that it is not an altered state of consciousness at all, as the shaman knows it, but rather it is a paradigm shift of awareness that is empty of all notions of a subjective self and dualist conditionings. In doing this we will see that the altered states of the shaman maintain a dualistic conception of reality despite the fact that it is a privileged perspective in relation to the average citizen in society. This state of *unconditioned consciousness*, which is the goal of Buddhist Tantra, is void of the subject-object experience, which shamans require in order to fulfill their duties associated with the community.

This project intends to point out the distinction between the dualist and nondualist positions and show that the *authentic* goal of tantric practice serves to undermine both the

---

[4] Madhyamaka Buddhism, while not itself a nondualist philosophical system, contains the notion of enlightenment as a nondualist principle of experience arising at the final stages. Significantly, it is the notion of enlightenment itself which I wish to employ in the text above and not specifically the philosophical systems of Madhyamaka or Yogacara Buddhism.

dualistic and the shamanistic worldviews. Further, while this in no way denies the value of the shaman within the mainstream of Tibetan Buddhist society, it establishes the limit inherent in the shaman's altered states of conscious-ness. Equating the dualistic aims of Tibetan Shamanic Buddhism, as Samuel does, with the nondualist goals of enlightenment for a tantric practitioner will clearly demonstrate what is classically defined as a category mistake.

Clerical Buddhism:
The Goal of Enlightenment and Nondualism

The Buddhist notion of enlightenment is a difficult subject to grasp. The difficulty often lies in the fact that a typical human sensory experience of the world is dualistic (subject-object viewpoint) and, therefore, obstructive to the acceptance of a nondual perspective. Our analysis of the world is chiefly comprised of sense data – such as taste, sight, and touch – which registers within the dimensional limitations of physical existence. Whatever reality is, it is primarily *experienced* by human sensory equipment as a *physical* reality. Any movement from this perspective involves a form of imaginative mental activity and discipline to override our sense inputs. Furthermore, to even 'think' about nondualism presents particular problems. Thoughts are fragments of experience and, while they can be assembled together in such a way as to form a coherent concept, they remain nothing more than a fragmented reflection or facsimile of reality and can never give the experience of nondualism itself. All thoughts are constructed of memory and, therefore, *as long as 'thoughts' are being utilised to investigate nondualism one can never achieve a state of nondualism, in the moment, as a direct experience.* The individual will only directly experience the thoughts, memories or concepts about nonduality; never the actual state of nonduality itself.

An exploration of nonduality lies at the heart of the Mahayana Buddhist endeavour and its chief proponents argued extensively about the irrationality of our senses when engaging in ontological problems. One of the greatest expressions of the nondual notion of reality came from Nagarjuna, founder of the Madhyamaka school of Mahayana Buddhism. In his most well known work, *Mulamadhyamakarika*, Nagarjuna speaks of the incoherence of dualistic concepts and the incongruence of the conceptualisation of a self (subject) in the world (object). "If the self were to be identical with the aggregates, it will partake of uprising and ceasing [and thereby be impermanent, unreal]. If it were to be different from the aggregates, it would have the characteristics of the non-aggregates [not-knowable]."[5] In this passage, Nagarjuna illustrates the impermanence of any potential 'self' which either is formed from out of impermanent qualities (the aggregates or *skandhas*) or as arising from something unknowable to us. As David J. Kalupahana explains:

> Nagarjuna has not given any indication that he recognizes a special intuitive faculty through which one can see beyond the world of change

---

[5] David J. Kalupahana, *Mulamadhyamakarika of Nagarjuna: The Philosophy of the Middle Way.* (Delhi: Moti-lal Banarsidass Publishers, 1986), 263.

and impermanence. Indeed, all that he has admitted points to his recognition of sense experiences as the foundation of human knowledge. The impermanent aggregates constitute not only the human personality, but also its experiences. If the self is considered to be different from the aggregates, Nagarjuna is here implying that it is unknowable, not merely inconceivable, for it will not have any of the characteristics of the aggregates that are all that we know through sense experience.[6]

This 'unknowable' is the goal of tantric practice and is the result that all serious tantric practitioners seek to attain. It is unknowable in that enlightenment cannot be conceived of prior to its occurrence, nor can it be described or 'thought about' in a conceptual 'form' once achieved. Nagarjuna's argument denies the substantiality of holding to a conceptual or sensual framework of reality. Anything arising or existing out of the characteristics of the five aggregates remains within the realm of duality and is, in his framework, illusory. This is the first major blow against a shamanistic endeavour, which seeks to work in the human realm through the spiritual realm. Where the shaman's experience is specifically dualistic in nature, within a subject-object framework of reality, Nagarjuna suggests that true reality – or enlightenment, as an experience of that reality – exists outside of the constraints of the *skandhas* altogether. Nondualism is not merely seeing the world as one interconnected world of subjects

---

[6] Kalupahana, 263-64.

and objects but that it cannot be conceived of at all in any terms.

The intended consequence of tantric practice, as an extinction of 'self', is further described by Nagarjuna: "In the absence of a self, how can there be something which belongs to the self? From the appeasing of the modes of self and selfhood, one abstains from creating notions of 'mine' and 'I'."[7] Nagarjuna is moving steadily toward a complete repudiation of a 'self' in any term that can be known or pre-conceived by the individual through his familiar modes of perception and experience. Kalupahana further elucidates:

> If a permanent entity does not exist, one cannot assume the existence of anything that belongs to it. The denial of a permanent entity does not mean that Nagarjuna is committed to a rejection of self-awareness or self-consciousness. The rejection of the latter would undermine the very foundation of his epistemology.... Nagarjuna, following the Buddha, recognized consciousness (and this includes self-awareness), not as a pre-existent *cogito*, but as part of the human personality conditioned by factors such as the sense organs and the objects of perception.... The result is the 'construction of a self' (*aham + kara*),[8] which eventually leads to the belief in permanence.[9]

The approach by Nagarjuna maintains its strength by showing that illusions about reality arise through any perceptions registered through the context of an 'I', which is in itself illusory.

---

[7] Kalupahana, 264.
[8] Literally "I-making."
[9] Kalupahana, 264.

Where any notion of a subjective or experiencing self exists, there too, reside illusions and a misinterpretation of reality. It is not so detrimental that the individual constructs a personality utilizing the *skandhas* but that the consciousness comes to *believe* that it *is* that personality and that experiences collected through that perspective are accurate interpretations of reality. This belief constitutes the chains that bind the individual to *samsara*. This also relegates the shaman's experiences to the realm of dualism. As such, the nondual experience of enlightenment is alien to the shaman in any measure. Stcherbatsky portrays Nagarjuna's position on the Absolute (Nirvana) as an end to all phenomenal existence; not actually – for that is an impossible claim to make – but experientially.[10] In the end, Nagarjuna leaves us without grounds to think about duality in any logically convincing way.

Yogacara's 'Mind-only' doctrine denies the absolute (ontological) existence of any autonomous or self-subsisting entity. From a perceptual (epistemological) standpoint, it represents "a powerful critique against (1) the objectification of language, (2) the artificiality of dualistic logic, and (3) the types of conventional knowledge derived from both."[11] That is, the 'Mind-only' doctrine acts as a critique against the belief in a dualistic interpretation of the world.

---

[10] Stcherbatsky, Theodore. *The Conception of Buddhist Nirvana*. (New York: Gordon Press, 1973), 5-6.
[11] Florin Giripescu Sutton. *Existence and Enlightenment in the Lankavatara-sutra: A Study in the Ontology and Epistemology of the Yogacara School of Mahayana Buddhism*. (Albany: State University of New York Press, 1991), xvii.

Therefore, what we see of the world (as a dualistic playground of subjects and objects) and the language we use to describe those objects cannot be translated into an absolute declaration about the true nature of the world. Conventional knowledge referred to in the quote above also represents the conceptualising faculties of an individual as well as the field of perception through which the shaman depends upon to function in his duties. It, again, is constructed of thoughts, which are fragmented instances of memory.

> This kind of knowledge...is really no knowledge, since it can only provide the delusion of facticity, or the 'Suchness' of things, tainted as it is by the subjective factors of perception and biased judgment. True knowledge [enlightenment], on the other hand, can only be attained within the context of the *totality* of human existence, that is to say, in the direct experience of life, which transcends verbal categories, dual logic, and pseudo-ontology based upon the reification of thoughts and ideas (including the idea of Mind-only itself!).[12]

Vasubandhu, the 4th century Yogacaric philosopher, attempts to assert a positive view of nondualism. In his commentaries on *The Separation of the Middle From Extremes* (*Madhyanata-Vibhaga-Bhasya*) he states that,

> Consciousness arises as the appearance of objects of the senses and of understanding, and as the appearance of sentient beings, self, and

---

[12] Sutton, xvii-xviii.

perceptions. There is no (real) object for it, and in its non-being, it itself is not.[13]

In Vasubandhu's commentaries we see the move to a more positive statement about the nature of reality in relation to our ability to perceive that reality. As we perceive objects in the world (receive sensory input), we create a subjective 'self' in response. Individual consciousness becomes conditioned through the impact of the environment on the senses as well as with our examination and identification with those experiences. The impact and recording of an object gives rise to a 'subject that is recording' and thus our sense of duality, however illusory, is created and intensified. Giuseppe Tucci renders an interpretation of the Yogacara philosophy, inspired by Maitreya through Asanga, by saying that "mysticism cannot but be monistic, and the system of Maitreya is chiefly mystic."[14] This is clearly illustrated in Asanga's primary works, *The Lankavatara Sutra*. Here we see that a further illusion exists in treating Nirvana (enlightenment) as an object of attainment itself.

> Some philosophers conceive nirvana to be found where a system of mentation no more operates owing to the cessation of the Skandhas, Dhatus, and Ayatanas, or to the indifference to

---

[13] Stefan Anacker, *Seven Works of Vasubandhu: The Buddhist Psychological Doctor*. (Delhi: Motilal Banarsidass Publishers, 1984), 212.
[14] Giuseppe Tucci, *On Some Aspects of the Doctrines of Maitreya[natha] and Asanga*. (Calcutta: University of Calcutta, 1930, 27.

the objective world, or to the recognition that all things are impermanent;...
When it is not thoroughly understood that there is nothing but what is seen of the Mind itself, dualistic determinations take place; when it is thoroughly understood that there is nothing but what is seen of the Mind itself, discrimination ceases.[15]

Nirvana is described here as being something even less than the subtlest of mind states. It is in actually seeing that all experience occurs strictly as a function of the Mind itself, and that to even think or conceptualise about our experiences in any way, that individual consciousness remains ensnared within the dualistic notion of reality. The Shamanic Buddhist, as a result, must deal with an enhanced multitude of objects, both in the material and the spiritual realm.

The 'state' of enlightenment, if such a misleading description is permitted, is only perceived when the object-discriminating activity of the mind ceases. For the practitioner, duality ceases to be, along with any conception or activity as a subjective 'self.' The experience itself is nondual and can never logically be the goal of the Shamanic Buddhist who must necessarily remain engaged with a dualistic experience of the world, albeit a much expanded and privileged conception of the world.

To achieve enlightenment is to actually extinguish the very activity that substantiates the subjective role and identity of the shaman interacting with his objective community. To think in terms of the shaman as engaged in a

---

[15] D. T. Suzuki, *The Lankavatara Sutra*. (London: Routledge and Kegan Paul Ltd., 1966), 158-61.

search for enlightenment in any way is to misunderstand the epistemological issues surrounding enlightenment. In other words, the goal of tantric practice is to achieve a nondualistic state of mind (i.e. enlightenment) whereas the goal of the shaman is to employ tantric methods to extend his dualistic perspective beyond merely the physical realm and into the spiritual realm.

**Shamanic Buddhism:
Altered States of Consciousness and Dualism**

A variety of definitions have been attempted to describe the position and phenomenon of shaman. Samuel states that, within Tibetan culture, shamanic training often arises out of the Vajrayanic tradition. "The Vajrayana's technique for obtaining Buddhahood function in practical terms as a means of training shamanic practitioners. Lamas in Tibet function as shamans, and they do so through the techniques and practices of Vajrayana Buddhism."[16] If we are to accept this statement that the use of tantra in shamanic training can be considered a *practical* application, then it seems to imply that striving to obtain Buddhahood or enlightenment may be an impractical notion. More likely, however, is that the severe difficulty in attaining enlightenment makes it more common that practitioners will utilise tantric methods for unintended purposes including the altering of one's own state of consciousness. This also

---

[16] Samuel, 9.

suggests that the goals of Shamanic and Clerical Buddhists are not equally motivated toward enlightenment but that the former remain in *samsara* while broadening their influence there through tantra. This is *contrary* to tantric belief and practice.

The central focus of tantric yoga is on enlightenment, using a system of techniques designed to break down the subject's sense of a separate identity. One of these central techniques involves the process of identifying oneself with one or another of the Vajrayanic deities in the hope of embodying those energies or qualities represented by the deity. In the meantime, one's own identity is annihilated or extinguished in the process. "The Vajrayana mythologizes the doctrine of emptiness, and teaches that the adept, through a combination of rites, is reinstated into his true *diamond-nature*."[17] Samuel states that the primary mode of activity of Shamanic Buddhism is in the use of *analogy* and *metaphor*.[18] The mythologizing of universal forces in Vajrayana Buddhism naturally fits it for use by the shaman in their training. Their goal appears to be more pragmatic in relation to the world of daily affairs, however, than those Buddhist practitioners who are seeking enlightenment and release from *samsara*. To develop the grounds upon which Samuel bases his position, he provides a standard definition of his understanding of the term 'shamanic.'

---

[17] Edward Conze, *Buddhism: Its Essence and Development*. (New York: Harper Torchbooks, 1959), 178.
[18] Samuel, 15.

> I use the term 'shamanic' as a general term for a category of practices found in differing degrees in almost all human societies. This category of practices may be briefly described as *the regulation and transformation of human life and human society through the use (or purported use) of alternate states of consciousness by means of which specialist practitioners are held to communicate with a mode of reality alternative to, and more fundamental than, the world of everyday experience.*"[19]

This lucid statement on the position and activity of the shaman in Tibet provides us with a ground for Samuel's notion of Shamanic Buddhism. He continues by explaining that a particular distinction is to be made between the shaman involved in general Tibetan folk-religion – who employ spirit-mediums to communicate with local deities – and those Shamanic Buddhists who employ Vajrayanic techniques "centered around communication with an alternative mode of reality (that of the Tantric deities) via the alternate states of consciousness of Tantric yoga."[20] The common factor between the Tibetan shamans of folk-religion and Shamanic Buddhism is clearly that alternate states of consciousness are utilised in their role with Tibetan society. Both these states allow them to interact with various aspects of reality beyond the scope of the everyday experience of individuals in Tibetan society. The main difference seems to be that the Shamanic Buddhist communicates with a higher grade of

---

[19] Samuel, 8.
[20] Samuel, 8.

spirits as represented in the Vajrayana pantheon.

The question we need to ask, however, is do these altered states of the shaman, *as achieved through the particular effects, which the tantric techniques provide*, lead also to enlightenment as Samuel suggests? That is, is the experience that the shaman engages in, the *actual* experience for which that tantric practice was originally intended? Answering such questions requires a closer look at the actual altered states themselves and to address the perspective(s) that they represent.

Mircea Eliade, a prominent scholar of the shamanic tradition, suggests that shamanism can be described as a *"technique of ecstasy."*[21] He adds to this notion by suggesting that the shaman additionally "specializes in a trance during which his soul is believed to leave the body and ascend to the sky or descend to the underworld."[22] The shaman is considered the master of the technique of ecstasy and through a specific technique rises to a state of awareness of the 'world of the spirits.' In this spirit world the shaman learns to deal with those forces influencing the daily affairs of the community or society. Whether dealing with the death of an individual – and the subsequent guidance of that soul to the 'other' world – or the manipulation of the 'elementals' responsible for promoting human discord or illness the shaman must enter into an ecstatic state of sorts in order to acquire

---

[21] Mircea Eliade. *Shamanism: Archaic Techniques of Ecstasy*. Translated by Willard R. Trask, (Princeton: Princeton University Press, 1964), 4.
[22] Eliade, 5.

skills in the spirit world. These skills are distinct, for instance, from those found in the role of magician.

> Shamanism exhibits a particular magical specialty...'mastery over fire,' 'magical flight,' and so on. By virtue of this fact though the shaman is, among other things, a magician, not every magician can properly be termed a shaman. The direction must be applied in regard to shamanic healing; every medicine man is a healer, but the shaman employs a method that is his and his alone. As for the shamanic techniques of ecstasy, they do not exhaust all the varieties of ecstatic experience documented in the history of religions and religious ethnology.[23]

So the Shamanic state of ecstasy is unique and extends beyond the limits of simple ecstatic experience but involves the ability to function *individually* within that experience and interact in such a way as to effect change. This signifies that the shaman has established some special *relation* to the 'spirits'. Those 'spirits' may turn out to be "the soul of a dead person, a 'nature spirit,' a mythical animal, and so on."[24] As Eliade interprets the skill of a shaman: "The shaman controls his 'spirits' in the sense that he, a human being, is able to communicate with the dead, 'demons,' and 'nature spirits,' without thereby becoming the instrument."[25] This is a clear assertion about the need for a shaman to maintain a dualistic perspective as well as some

---

[23] Eliade, 5.
[24] Eliade, 6.
[25] Eliade, 7.

form of subjective 'self' which is antagonistic to authentic tantric practice.

The shaman develops special relationships through the technique of ecstasy and uses those relationships to manipulate the unseen affairs of the world that affect the community. The achievement of these skills can take an enormous period of time – sometimes decades. The time required to master the training often depends upon the shaman's ability to master communication in the spirit world whilst maintaining a degree of personal safety or protection. As suggested by Spence L. Rogers, "the methods of the medicine man [shaman] show great variety. Each theory of disease calls for a different way of affecting the cure. Views as to the cause of disease vary with the culture area, with the tribe and, to some degree, with the medicine man himself."[26] Roger's statement speaks to the need of maintaining a distinct identity. Despite this variance, however, it is the shaman's altered state of awareness as an individual, which facilitates their diagnosis and treatment of illness. The shaman must interact with the spiritual world and work to make changes that ultimately affect the material side of experience. As such, the shaman *appears* to deal with the causes of events.

> Basically, the shaman's approach toward the universal forces is based on one or more of three fundamental assumptions. First, the essence of power is such that it can be controlled mechanically through incantations, formulas, and rituals. All of these may, with proper

---

[26] Spence L. Rogers, *The Shaman's Healing Way*. (Ramona: Acoma Books, 1976), 28.

technique and effort, be channeled in the direction intended: healing the sick, averting plague, dealing with astronomical peculiarities, or solving other problems of community concern. Second is the assumption that the universe is controlled by a mysterious power which can be directed through the meticulous avoidance of certain acts or through zealous observance of certain strict obligations toward persons, places, and objects. The third assumption is that the affairs of mankind are managed through the force and will of spirits, ghosts, and divinities, whose actions can be influenced by human effort.[27]

Rogers later points to the obvious factor that this third assumption presupposes the existence of spiritual beings that can be manipulated or directed under the instructions of a shaman.[28] As such, we see the shaman occupying some distinct subjective space, whether in this world or in the spiritual world. The shaman maintains a subjective state of existence in relation to a world, or realms, of objects. This dualistic experience of reality extends beyond merely their material experience and appears to accommodate their 'non-material' experiences too.

These 'non-material' experiences are often dependent upon, and function within, notions or beliefs about the cosmological make-up of the universe. As Schlesier states, the Tsistsistas shamans (Cheyenne) "acted on the highest level of achievement possible to humans in the frame of a world description that they originally

---

[27] Spence L. Rogers, *The Shaman: His Symbols and His Healing Power*. (Springfield: Charles C Thomas Publishers, 1982), 43.
[28] Rogers, *Symbols*, 44.

formulated long ago."[29] The field of experience for the shaman is determined by their, essentially, mythological framework of the universe. The shaman creates a blueprint of the material and non-material universe that he enters either by trance or ecstatic experience. Similarly, with the Ojibway, "as the shamanic ritual evolves from the shaman's initiating experience, the formative encounter with the *manitou*[30] provides the central symbols with which the shaman dramatically re-enacts his vocational call."[31] The realm required for this interaction is established on the Ojibway cosmological order. "The concept of the multilayered earth is a recurring theme in Ojibway shamanism. Through this symbol of the mysterious regions of the universe, the Ojibway shaman structures his communication with *manitou* power."[32] The shaman is not only restricted to a dualist experience of the world but also to his conceptually constructed belief about the constitution of the universe. This cosmological framework, accessible in part only through trance, establishes the ring-pass-not for the shaman's activities.

If we look closer at the altered state of awareness known as *trance* we see an interesting

---

[29] Karl H Schlesier, *The Wolves of Heaven: Cheyenne Shamanism, Ceremonies, and Prehistoric Origins.* (Norman: University of Oklahoma Press, 1987), 6.

[30] John A Grim, *The Shaman: Patterns of Siberian and Ojibway Healing.* (Norman: University of Oklahoma Press, 1983) 6. "Among the Algonguian peoples of North America, *manitou*...encompasses a wide variety of spirit presences."

[31] Grim, 138.

[32] Grim, 78.

phenomenon arise. According to Wolfgang G. Jilek,

> The term trance designates a 'state of double consciousness, i.e., the constricted state of awareness of the personal self which co-exists with the dream-like state of consciousness of the para-personal self.' The neuropsychological basis of any trance or possession state is the dissociation of the self, which loses its experiential unity and is converted into a secondary 'dual system of relational experience,' namely, the personal self and the para-personal self."[33]

Regardless of the particular 'world' in which the shaman's experience is functioning, there remains a dualist experience of subject-object relations. Within trance, the shaman undergoes a further fragmentation and a second para-personal self is 'constructed' to facilitate the shamanic encounters. This experience seems common to all descriptions of shamanic experience and the presence of some form of subjective 'self' seems not only incident to shamanic activity but also necessary. Despite a privileged interaction with other realms of existence, the shaman is still a subjective individual with a duty to fulfill. As such, the shaman cannot move beyond any form of experience that would additionally annihilate the shaman's conceptual framework of the universe and reality. Indeed, it would appear that the quality of the shamanic experience is highly

---

[33] Wolfgang G. Jilek, *Indian Healing: Shamanic Ceremonialism in the Pacific Northwest Today*. (Surrey: Hancock House Publishers, Ltd., 1982), 23.

dependent upon socio-cultural variables and the shaman's relationship to those variables.

The capacity of attaining altered states of consciousness is a universal property of the human central nervous system as evidenced by the ubiquitous occurrence of trance phenomena through time and space. However, the prevalence of these phenomena appears to be a function of socio-cultural variables. Under the impact of rationalistic-positivistic ideologies, the normal faculty of manifesting with psychogenic dissociation appears to have diminished among members of the Western urban middle class who would nowadays not to be expected to readily enter into hysterical twilight reactions, daemoniac possessions, or religious frenzy, while these states are by no means rare in more tradition-oriented pockets of Western culture."[34]

Where we are not under the socio-cultural expectations to undergo trance, it appears that capacity to attain this state diminishes. This last statement is important for many reasons as it provides for the distinction between the differences in experience achieved by the shamanic use of tantric exercises. In the same way that the rationalistic ideology of the West tends to deter its citizens from achieving the disassociative trance state, the shaman's cosmological worldview *obligates* them toward these trance states, which may preclude them from achieving any true nondual state of enlightenment. Shamanic Buddhists reinforce their dual notion of reality by manifesting this quality of experience into realms not normally available to other members of the community. To

---

[34] Jilek, 24.

shamanic practitioners, the spirit realm is also dual in nature. On the other hand, Clerical Buddhists, at least those with the Bodhi orientation,[35] seek a nondual experience of reality and employ the tantric methods strictly toward that end. They do not seek the spiritual realm, *per se*, but attempt to annihilate all dualistic conceptualisations of reality.

This dichotomy is most obviously illustrated in *The Tibetan Book of the Dead*. Known originally as *Liberation Through Understanding in the Between*, this text exemplifies the distinction between the Shamanic and Tantric goals. The consciousness, which remains immediately after the death of the individual, is guided through several stages in an attempt to achieve liberation from *samsara*. The initial stages immediately following death offer the best opportunities for the consciousness to see that all experience is simply the activity of the Mind. If this recognition occurs then the illusion of *samsara* is seen and the individual achieves Liberation. However, if the individual consciousness fails to recognize this then it remains trapped in illusion and requires subsequent guidance through the many illusory states of experience. The hope is to lead the consciousness in a way which will establish the best opportunity for reincarnation; that being dependent upon the final state of experience which the consciousness 'adheres' itself to.

> The Between is after all a time of crisis after death, when the soul (the very subtle mind-body) is in its most highly formed fluid state. Naturally

---

[35] Samuel describes the Bodhi Orientation as a philosophical orientation toward achieving Enlightenment.

much of the art of Tantra is designed to work with precisely that totally transformable subtle state.... This is indeed why the between-traveler can become instantly liberated just by understanding where he or she is in the between, what the reality is, where the allies are, and where the dangers are."[36]

As Thurman shows, the tantric practitioner is concerned with liberation and freedom from the experience of identity and, thus, from duality and *samsara*. The recently deceased individual is led through the variety of encounters with various 'gods' and 'demons' to which the Shamanic Buddhist normally has access. It is the privilege of the trained Shamanic Buddhist to commonly interact amongst the spirit realm which ordinary individuals only now encounter upon their actual physical death and release from the body. As a result of the newly deceased failing to initially let go of a dualistic mental prison, the shamanic guide tries to produce the best of all possible outcomes for the consciousness that remains trapped within the dualist experience of mind. Having bypassed the opportunity for liberation and escape from *samsara*, it remains to struggle with the subsequent opportunities for a fortunate rebirth within *samsara*.

Samuel continues by arguing that the Buddhist's rejection of the involvement with daily communal and societal concerns is an important part of shamanic training. "Shamans have to be able to 'go beyond' these [social] patterns and attain a degree of impartiality to them in order to

---

[36] *The Tibetan Book of the Dead*, Translated by Robert F. Thurman. (New York: Bantam Books, 1994), 80.

carry out their mediatory and manipulatory function in relation to patterns."[37] Eliade, likewise, suggests strong parallels between yogic tantra techniques and the techniques of shamanism.[38] However, while the techniques may appear similar, their intents and aims are enormously dissimilar. Where the shamanic technique seeks to gain control over a broader range of 'realms' in a dualistic perspective of the world, the Tantric yogi seeks a permanent death of the psychological self and any subject-object distinctions whatsoever.

It should be clear at this point that the altered state sought for by the Shamanic Buddhist emphasizes a dualist perspective of reality; this in the form of a greatly expanded concept of reality which experientially includes the 'spiritual realm'. This emphasis requires that they 'die' to any preconceived notion of a physical self but maintain, or even expand upon, the concept of a certain psychological para-personal 'self,' which possesses movement and influence across a broader experience of reality. While they expand the range of themselves as a subject they also *reinforce* their experience of themselves as a subject. This perpetuates and accents the dualist perspective.

With the ground covered to this point it is possible to pictorially examine the notions described here. One of the most lucid illustrations of this point in Tibetan Buddhist philosophy can be found in the *Wheel of Life*. In this symbolic illustration we see Yama, the great Lord of Illusion, holding the wheel in his grip.

---

[37] Samuel, 371.
[38] Eliade, 436-38.

The wheel represents *samsara* – the world of illusion and duality – and Yama sustains the illusions to which sentient beings within the circle have succumbed. Outside the wheel stands the Buddha representing the path to enlightenment and freedom from the illusion of subject-object duality. Within the wheel we find the six realms of existence including regions of hell, heaven, hungry ghosts, animals, humans, and the titans or demi-gods. The shaman functions within these realms and gains the mobility to move between each realm in service of those whose conscious awareness remains confined solely to the realm of humans. But the shaman cannot move outside of the *Wheel of Life* itself; they are no more intrinsically free from *samsara* than any other particular being. The shaman remains embedded within the wheel as any other resident of *samsara* although they may have a greater freedom to move within the wheel. In no way does this ability to move across the different realms advance the shaman's perspective in any way that would fit them to step outside of that dualistic category of perception. In fact, the ability to move amongst the different realms may serve only to reinforce the epistemological convictions of dualism.

It should be clear from this analysis, therefore, that the goals of the Shamanic Buddhist and the Clerical Buddhist differ significantly and to draw any parallel would constitute a category mistake. While each employs tantric techniques in their training, the Shamanic Buddhist employs tantric techniques to break down the barriers between realms *within* a dualistic conception of the world and this reinforces their perception of themselves as a subject. On the other hand, the Clerical Buddhist employs tantric practices in order to break down dualist perceptions of the world altogether and seeks to transcend *samsara* (dualism) entirely.

Conclusion

The ideas we have explored here are, at times, difficult to grasp in their entirety. This is due mainly to the problems inherent in talking about nondualism and the condition of Nirvana or enlightenment. In developing a comparison to the shaman's dualistic (altered) states of consciousness it was necessary to provide a conception or understanding of nondualism. But nondualism does not lend itself well to conceptualisation. It cannot even be said to be antithetical to, or the opposite of, dualism as that only serves to make nondualism another feature or conceptualisation within the realm of dualistic thinking. Nondualism is a 'state of awareness' wherein the characteristically fragmented presence of thought, memory, and conceptualisation are absent altogether. In this respect, nondualism cannot be 'thought about' in any 'absolute' manner, but can only be accurately perceived when it is experienced directly in the moment.

My approach involved showing the incoherence of dualism as illustrated through Mahayana Buddhism. Tantra, as a method intended *exclusively* for achieving enlightenment, can be seen as a technique designed to progressively penetrate through the illusion of a dualistic perception of the world leading to the annihilation of a subjective form of 'self'.

However, shamans are necessarily dualistic in their outlook in order to fulfill their goal of establishing harmony and balance in the community. Therefore, Shamanic Buddhists borrow limited forms of tantric practice in order to weaken their notion of a personal 'self' in order to be able to re-construct and instantiate the use of a para-personal 'self' for use across a broader aspect of the dualist cosmos. This can be seen to function in a contradictory manner to the true intended purpose of tantric practice, which is Enlightenment and Liberation from *samsara*. The Shamanic Buddhist seeks to simply extend their conscious awareness within what is for them a broader manifestation of *samsara*. The Clerical Buddhist seeks a nondualistic perspective and the complete annihilation of all notions of 'self' through tantric practice. The fact that these altered states are facilitated through the application of some tantric techniques does not justify Samuel in equating these as possessing the common goal of enlightenment. Samuel has made a *category mistake* in making the goals of dualistic and nondualistic perceptions commensurate. As we have come to understand, the enlightened state is in no way directly comparable to the altered or trance states of ecstasy sought by the Shamanic Buddhists.

Ramana Maharshi: The Light of Advaita Vedanta

> He who experiences the unity of life
> sees his own Self in all beings...
> —*Buddha*

Chief amongst the texts that comprise the *Vedic* tradition are the *Upanishads*. David R. Kinsley states that "for a great many Hindus, the essence of their tradition is found in the *Upanishads*, which traditionally are called *Vedanta* (the end or goal of knowledge). In the *Upanishads* a central concern is the self-discovery of the ground and origin of reality."[1] Kinsley offers an example of the Upanishadic philosophical tradition in the modern South Indian saint Ramana Maharshi wherein "Ramana's teachings and his path...may be taken as representative of thousands of anonymous spiritual adepts over the centuries who have sought self-knowledge in [Vedantic] Hinduism."[2] The Upanishadic technique of teaching or imparting understanding in a way that leaves the seeker in a position of discovering truths within themselves requires a special insight into the nature of reality. As Kinsley's praise suggests, Maharshi's life expressed this insight, and the form of his teaching warrants a more detailed examination. For the purpose of this essay I thought it would be interesting to

---

[1] David R. Kinsley, *Hinduism: A Cultural Perspective*. (Englewood Cliffs: Prentice Hall, 1993), 47.
[2] Kinsley, 48.

explore some of the characteristics and episodes from Ramana Maharshi's life and expression in order to illustrate how he represented that search for self-knowledge. That is, I will attempt to show that Ramana Maharshi both taught and embodied in his actions many of the core principles of the *Advaita Vedanta*.[3]

Sri Ramana Maharshi was born under the name of Venkataraman in the South Indian town Tiruchuzhi on December 29, 1879. This date is auspicious for many Hindus and, in particular, devotees of Siva. It marks the event of Arudra Darshan or 'Sight of Siva' and commemorates "the occasion when Siva manifested Himself to his devotees as Nataraja."[4] For this reason, many of the Maharshi's later devotees came to see him as an Avatar or incarnation of Siva. As a young boy he displayed few natural mental skills apart from his amazing abilities in retention.[5] The only unusual characteristics of any notoriety were his abnormal sleeping patterns which ranged from states of absolute deep sleep to states of half-sleep throughout the night. Maharshi recounts stories from his youth of episodes of deep sleep:

---

[3] *Advaita Vedanta* is a particular interpretation of the Upanishadic philosophy that expresses the notion that the true Self, or Atman, is unconditionally one with Brahman, the Universal Whole. This perspective, held by Ramana Maharshi, consists of an entirely monistic view of Reality.
[4] Arthur Osborne, *Ramana Maharshi and the Path of Self-Knowledge*. (London; Rider and Company, 1970), 13.
[5] Osborne, 15. Osborne actually characterizes the young Venkataraman as generally unfocused and somewhat lazy with "no sign of his ever becoming a scholar."

> The boys didn't dare touch me when I was awake but if they had any grudge against me they would come when I was asleep and carry me wherever they liked and beat me as much as they liked and then put me back and I would know nothing about it until they told me next morning.[6]

These periods of intense sleep contrasted other periods when he would experience lucid half-sleep states. Arthur Osborne, Ramana's biographer, describes this latter unique quality as characteristic of highly advanced adepts and is indicative of "the ability to observe oneself objectively as a witness."[7] This 'wakefulness', as we will come to see, was also to become the essential theme in his later teachings. Despite this, however, Maharshi's life remained relatively uneventful until the age of sixteen – a time described as one of revelation and enlightenment for the young Venkataraman.

In the *Katha Upanishad* we read that the stage of a 'knower of Brahman' cannot be achieved through mere knowledge but by the grace of God:

> That Self cannot be gained by the Veda, not by understanding, nor by much learning. He whom the Self chooses, by him the Self can be gained. The Self chooses him (his body) as his own.[8]

The events surrounding Ramana Maharshi's enlightenment parallel this description from the

---

[6] Osborne, 15.
[7] Osborne, 16.
[8] Max Müller, ed., *Sacred Books of the East Series: The Upanishads, Part II*. Translated by Max Müller. (Delhi: Motilal Banarsidass, 1965), 11.

Upanishads and appear as every bit a result of the 'grace of God' than by any specific technique or prolonged practice. At the age of sixteen, Ramana was profoundly affected after reading the *Periapuranam* – a book containing the life stories of the sixty-three Tamil saints. This seemed to trigger in him a mysterious process described by others as an awakening "current of awareness."[9] Ramana, himself, said, "at first I thought it was some kind of fever but I decided, if so, it is a pleasant fever, so let it stay."[10] A short time later, he was sitting alone when he was suddenly struck with a violent fear of death. The shock of the experience drove him inwards to mentally confront the devastating fear. Assuming the position of a deceased corpse, he laid down rigid on the ground with limbs stretched out and held his breath. He later described the revelation that followed:

> 'Well then,' I said [to] myself, 'this body is dead. It will be carried stiff to the burning ground and there burnt to ashes. But with the death of this body am I dead? Is the body I? It is silent and inert but I feel the full force of my personality and even the voice of the 'I' within me, apart from it. So I am Spirit transcending the body. The body dies but the Spirit that transcends it cannot be touched by death. That means I am the deathless Spirit.' All this was not dull thought; it flashed through me vividly as living truth which I perceived directly, almost without thought-process. "I" was something very real, the only real thing about my present state,.... From that moment onwards the 'I' or Self, focused attention on itself by a powerful fascination. Fear of death

---

[9] Osborne, 17.
[10] Osborne, 17.

had vanished once for all. Absorption in the Self continued unbroken from that time on....Previous to that crisis I had no clear perception of my Self and was not consciously attracted to it, much less any inclination to dwell permanently in it.[11]

By all accounts, Ramana Maharshi, without any significant prior exploration into the nature of Self, had attained the experience described in the *Upanishads* as the ground and origin of reality. As we have seen in the previous quote, Ramana described this sense of the Ultimate as a "living truth...perceived directly, almost without thought-process."[12] This reality of Spirit, lying behind the activity of the mind and thoughts, is aptly described for us in the *Katha Upanishad*.

> Beyond the senses is the mind, beyond the mind is the highest (created) Being, higher than that Being is the Great Self, higher than the Great, the highest Undeveloped.[13]

Also, in the *Kena Upanishad*, we read this reference to Spirit:

> There the eye goes not, nor words, nor mind. We know not, we cannot understand, how he can be explained. He is above the known and He is above the unknown.... What cannot be thought with the mind, but that whereby the mind can think: know That alone to be Brahman, the Spirit...[14]

---

[11] Prem Lata, *Mystic Saints of India: Shri Ramana Maharshi.* (New Delhi: Summit Publications,1986), 9.
[12] Lata, 9.
[13] Müller, *Upanishads, Part II*, 22.
[14] Juan Mascaro, *The Upanishads.* (London: Penguin Books, 1965), 51.

The experience described by Ramana Maharshi clearly embodied the notions portrayed in these Upanishadic verses. Beyond the classifying and discriminating abilities of the mind, suggested Maharshi, rests a conscious experiential state of the true Self as Spirit. With this in mind, he provided an account of the relationship existing between the ego or personality (constructed of thoughts in the mind) and the consciousness that underlies and animates that ego. From his deep insight into this inner relationship, Ramana elaborated upon a method through which others might experience this same truth. Although his own enlightenment had occurred in a short period of time, he saw the need for a method through which others could pursue this truth. His principle method offered was to pursue the enquiry, 'Who am I'.[15] By negating the various notions that constantly arose in the mind to construct an image of the 'I', an individual follows back along this thread to the source of 'I'. Eventually the 'I', too, vanishes and one experiences the true Self (pure unqualified consciousness) which is the real nature of the human being. Ramana felt that it would require a great mental effort for most individuals but that it was "the one infallible means, the only direct one, to realize the unconditioned, absolute Being that you really are."[16] He maintained that this internal enquiry

---

[15] *The Collected Works of Ramana Maharshi.* Edited by Arthur Osborne. (York Beach: Samuel Weiser, Inc., 1997). The main components of Ramana Maharshi's teaching can be found in two books, *Who Am I?* and *Self-Enquiry*, compiled from conversations with his devotees.
[16] Osborne, 21.

initiated a process of transmutation within the individual which would lead inevitably to the source of Self. The pursuit of this path is similarly reinforced in the *Mundaka Upanishad*:

> This Atman is attained by truth and *tapas* whence came true wisdom and chastity. The wise who strive and who are pure see him within the body in his pure glory and light.[17]

Here we see the *Vedic* injunction to strive relentlessly toward knowing the inner Self. Ramana's insight into the method of enquiry was meant to strike directly at the roots of ignorance within oneself. "The purpose of Self-enquiry is to focus the entire mind at its Source. It is not, therefore, a case of one 'I' searching for another 'I'."[18]

This instruction by Ramana Maharshi was intensely practical and he never answered metaphysical questions from devotees pertaining to such things as God or the afterlife. His response to these would often come in the form of "why do you want to know about God before you know yourself" or "why do you want to know what you will be when you die before you know what you are *now*?"[19] The only meaningful metaphysical enquiry, for Ramana, was to know the Self. In this point alone did the essence of the Upanishadic philosophy shine brightly in what was, for him, reality.

Ambiguity arose, at times, over his use of the terms 'I' and 'Self'. The term 'I' (in relation to others) suggested a sense of duality where none

---

[17] Muscaro, 80.
[18] Osborne, 149.
[19] Osborne, 83.

was obviously intended by Ramana. Instead, he meant to convey the notion that his experience of identity was that he *was* that Spirit which was in all things. Paul Brunton, a western seeker, rigorously questioned Ramana on the intricate notions of the 'Self' and the 'I'. He was informed by Ramana that one could trace back, step by step within oneself, to the origin of the 'I'-thought and that even that would vanish in time. The following dialogue illustrates what Maharshi claimed as the true nature of the human mind:

> *Brunton*: You mean it is possible to conduct such a mental investigation into oneself?
>
> *Sri Ramana*: Certainly. It is possible to go inwards until the last thought, 'I', gradually vanishes.
>
> *Brunton*: What is then left? Will a man then become quite unconscious or will he become an idiot?
>
> *Sri Ramana*: No; on the contrary, he will attain that consciousness which is immortal and he will become truly wise when he has awakened to his true Self, which is the real nature of man.
>
> *Brunton*: But surely the sense of 'I' must also pertain to that?
>
> *Sri Ramana*: The sense of 'I' pertains to the person, the body and brain. When a man knows his true Self for the first time something else arises from the depths of his being and takes possession of him. That something is beyond the mind; it is infinite, divine, eternal. Some people call it the Kingdom of Heaven, others call it the soul and others again Nirvana, and Hindus call it Liberation; you may give it what name you wish.

> When this happens a man has not really lost himself; rather he has found himself.
> Unless and until a man embarks on this quest of the true Self, doubt and uncertainty will follow his footsteps through life.... What is the use of knowing about everything else when you do not yet know who you are? Men avoid this enquiry into the true Self, but what else is there so worthy to be undertaken?[20]

In this exchange, Ramana Maharshi reveals a subtle but profound mystery behind the Upanishadic philosophy. In contrast to Brunton's concern that one's individuality is diminished or lost through Self-enquiry, Maharshi reveals, in fact, that one's individuality is not lost but, rather, expanded to Infinity. This explanation by Ramana gives a distinctly direct affirmation to verses found in the *Isa Upanishad*:

> Who sees all beings in his own Self, and his own Self in all beings, loses all fear. When a sage sees this great Unity and his Self *has become* all beings, what delusion and what sorrow can ever be near him?[21]

It can be seen that Ramana articulated a coherent interpretation for the above passage. One's individuality and identity was not annihilated but, instead, expanded to become all things. In essence, as a person came to discover their true Self, they not only understood the underlying unity in reality but came to actually experience and demonstrate it. Ramana attempted to clarify these points through personal one-on-one exchanges with those seeking answers

---

[20] Osborne, 20-1.
[21] Muscaro, 49.

from him. In true Upanishadic form, Ramana would sit in the presence of seekers, sometimes for days, and occasionally he would provide answers to profoundly complex questions.[22] Often Ramana would simply nod or respond with simple hand gestures. In many cases, he imparted the teaching silently to the student through a glance. In doing so, he demonstrated to the devotees the underlying truth of unity described in the *Upanishads*. Osborne recounts events illustrating the abilities Ramana Maharshi possessed in teaching silently to the devotees.

> Sri Bhagavan [Ramana] would turn to the devotee, his eyes fixed upon him with blazing intentness. The luminosity, the power of his eyes pierced into one, breaking down the thought-process. Sometimes it was as though an electrical current was passing through one, sometimes a vast peace, a flood of light. One devotee has described it: 'Suddenly Bhagavan turned his luminous, transparent eyes on me. Before that I could not stand his gaze for long. Now I looked straight back into those terrible, wonderful eyes, how long I could not tell. They held me in a sort of vibration distinctly audible to me.' Always it was followed by the feeling, the indubitable conviction, that one had been taken up by Sri Bhagavan, that henceforth he was in charge, he was guiding.[23]

Despite this internal sense of guidance by Ramana, however, he never admitted openly or directly to his role as guru. While he understood the relationship of Guru/devotee as existing in

---

[22] One interpretation of *Upanishad* is literally "to sit down beside" as in receiving teachings from a guru.
[23] Osborne, 144-5.

the minds and expectations of the disciples, no such relationship really existed for him. We are told that the universe, within Maharshi's mind, was experienced as one unified Being. Therefore, any notion of relationship would indicate duality. Maharshi explained this in a conversation with an English disciple, Major Chadwick:

> The guru or *Gnani* (Enlightened One) sees no difference between himself and others. For him all are *Gnani*, all are one with himself, so how can a *Gnani* say that such and such is his disciple? But the unliberated one sees all as multiple, he sees all as different from himself, so to him the Guru-disciple relation is a reality, and he needs the Grace of the Guru to waken him to Reality.[24]

Throughout his life he followed the renunciant's path and this was no more clearly demonstrated than at his death. Illness befell him during the last years of his life and there were attempts by his disciples to provide a cure for his tumours. Ramana refused prolonged treatment, though, and paid little attention to the illness or the pain it caused him. "There is no cause for alarm," he said, "the body itself is a disease; let it have its natural end. Why mutilate it? Simple dressing of the part is enough."[25] On April 14th, 1950, Ramana Maharshi passed away with the look of "indescribable tenderness" on is face.[26]

As we have seen, the life and teachings of Ramana Maharshi embodied many core concepts of the Upanishadic philosophy. Looking at the

---

[24] Osborne, 141-2.
[25] Osborne, 180.
[26] Osborne, 186.

periods surrounding his enlightenment and death, as well as his doctrine of Self-enquiry, it is clear how he expressed this reality to others and lived his life within that reality. While this essay is by no means a complete or comprehensive account of Ramana Maharshi's life, I have shown that particular highlights from his life appeared to demonstrate a direct insight into the nature of reality as described in the *Upanishads*. The essential position of the Upanishadic philosophy describes the true nature of Reality as a field of pure consciousness, or *Being*, which gives rise to the various thought-processes in humans. Ramana Maharshi's life expression exhibited characteristics of an awareness which extended well beyond the boundaries of a separate personal 'I'. This extension was demonstrated often in his ability to speak from this monistic perspective. Moreover, he delineated a method of enquiry for others designed to move the participant beyond their own thought processes. His teaching, therefore, cut right to the heart of the Upanishadic Philosophy. This is most directly summed up for us in the words of Ramana Maharshi himself: "All thoughts are inconsistent with Realization. The right thing to do is to exclude thoughts of oneself and all other thoughts. Thought is one thing and Realization is quite another."[27] In this we have the spirit of Vedanta expressed in a simple, straight-forward manner. It is clear then how the light of Advaita Vedanta emanated through the life of Ramana Maharshi. His encouragement for seekers to strive relentlessly at self-awareness embodied the true Advaitic spirit.

---

[27] Osborne, 151-2.

Questioning Coercive Institutions from a Confucian Perspective

> Heaven means to be one with God.
> —*Confucius*

Western political philosophers often provide social, political and economic models which are based entirely in western cultural values and experiences. If too narrowly conceived, these perspectives can often be seen as morally indefensible when removed from western contexts or examined through non-western perspectives. In his work *Contemporary Social and Political Philosophy* James P. Sterba provides his 'moral conclusion' that any legitimate social/political/economic system is one which satisfies the conditions of a basic-needs minimum for its citizens. In his view, "a basic-needs approach to specifying an acceptable minimum would guarantee people the goods and resources necessary to meet at least the normal costs of satisfying their basic needs in the society in which they live."[1] Moreover, Sterba asserts that, in all cases, permanent coercive institutions (i.e., law enforcement agencies, armies, etc.) are *required* in order to sustain these systems.[2] However, it is questionable whether this position is morally defensible when viewed through other lenses. It is conceivable that some perspectives

---

[1] James P. Sterba, *Contemporary Social and Political Philosophy*. (Wadsworth Publishing Company: Belmont, California. 1995), 17.
[2] Sterba, *Contemporary Social*, 110.

may provide a challenge to this assertion. Rather than requiring permanent coercive institutions to sustain basic-needs minimums in society, other views or approaches, such as that provided through Confucian philosophy, might prove that a compassionate and generous leadership in a nation could provide lasting conditions for peace and security. Indeed, I intend to show that Confucian philosophy morally supports both the notion of basic-needs minimums for the citizens as well as providing for this without the need for permanent coercive institutions.

Sterba begins his line of reasoning by adopting the *original position* stance defended by John Rawls.[3] Essentially, the original position is one in which we make choices about the allocation of resources in society "as though we were [all] standing behind an imaginary 'veil of ignorance' with respect to most particular facts about ourselves [and each other] – anything that would bias our choice or stand in the way of unanimous agreement."[4] Not knowing whether we would occupy a position of advantage or disadvantage in society we would, at least theoretically, be fairer in our allocation of social resources. Sterba continues from this position and analyses three common social distribution systems – maximin, utilitarian, and compromise views[5] – and shows that they are not sufficient to ensure the welfare of all when the original position is extended to include distant peoples

---

[3] John A. Rawls, *A Theory of Justice*. (Cambridge: Harvard University Press, 1971). Chapter 2.
[4] Sterba, *Contemporary Social*, 12-13.
[5] Sterba, *Contemporary Social*, 12-14. Sterba provides a detailed analysis of each viewpoint.

and future generations. Instead, Sterba demonstrates that the proviso of a 'basic-needs minimum' is necessary to accomplish these goals because, "if not satisfied, lead to significant lacks and deficiencies with respect to a standard of mental and physical well-being."[6] He defines this notion of basic-needs as "a person's needs for food, shelter, medical care, protection, companionship, and self-development."[7] To achieve these ends, however, he insists upon the use of force, relative to the resistance encountered, in order to establish and enforce a correct redistribution of resources.

> ...when one considers the degree of redistribution that would be necessary to achieve a basic-needs minimum within our own society and in the world at large, it is hard to see how coercive institutions could be avoided. Of course, the degree to which coercive institutions would be required would depend on the level and type of opposition that existed to achieving a basic-needs minimum. Other things being equal, the greater the opposition to securing and maintaining such a social minimum, the greater the need for coercive institutions.[8]

He goes on to test his views against many diverse styles of western political thought and arrives at the conclusion that it remains morally defensible to require coercive institutions in all cases. It is from this reasoning he is able to assert that, from all viewpoints, it is morally defensible to apply the standard of a basic-needs

---

[6] Sterba, *Contemporary Social*, 15.
[7] Sterba, *Contemporary Social*, 15.
[8] Sterba, *Contemporary Social*, 25.

minimum and that coercive institutions are required to sustain that standard. This may not be entirely true, however, as we investigate this assertion relative to political viewpoints and ideals outside western traditions. In so doing, we may come to see that Sterba's assertion regarding coercive institutions may be particular to western ways of thinking about society and social development.

To begin the analysis we will need to form some understanding of the foundations of Confucianism as provided in the *Analects*. The difficulty in doing this, though, lies in translating Chinese ethical terms into English. This occurs, for instance, in the word *jen* which arises as a term of philosophical importance in the *Analects*. The most common translation of *jen* is "humaneness" or "benevolence,"[9] and should be seen as a representation of an *innate* quality of the human being brought *into expression* (i.e., in relationship, person to person). In his exposition of Confucian philosophy, Raymond Dawson clarifies this idea:

> Basically *jen* means the manifestation of ideal human nature; and since Confucian ethics is concerned not so much with qualities of the mind and heart as with activities, and not so much with man in isolation as with man relating to his

---

[9] Raymond Dawson, *Confucius*. (London, England: Oxford University Press, 1981), 37. Raymond Dawson points out the difficulty of rendering the translation: "For *jen* nobody has found an entirely satisfactory solution. Benevolence, love, altruism, kindness, charity, compassion, magnanimity, perfect virtue, goodness, human-heartedness, humaneness, humanity, and man-to-manness have all been used."

fellow human beings, so that man's virtues are social virtues manifested in the conduct of human relationships, then *jen* may be defined as dealing with other human beings as a man ideally should...[T]he simplest description of *jen* in the *Analects* is that given in the reply to the disciple Fan Ch'ih, 'to love others.'[10]

So the ideal nature, which human beings should strive to locate and express in them, is 'to love others' and the expression that this entails becomes the *foundation* for culture. This description of love, however, is not complete without some further qualifications. F. C. Hsu takes exception to the 'flippant' rendering of *jen* as 'love,' and contends that it must be seen as something more than simple individual 'psychic love.'

> It is a cosmic principle called in Chinese 'the heart of Heaven and Earth,' that by which the Harmony of the universe manifests and pervades...[I]n other words, it is Divine Love... [and] it is *that* towards which every human being strives, and having attained it is then [themselves] divine. Descending more to the human level, it is that which every goodness is included... [A]ll in all, Jen is something that is rooted above and within, *an entity without which there can be no universe* [italics mine].[11]

The basic tenet of Confucian philosophy, then, lies in recognising the cosmic principle of Divine Love as a pervasive quality, innate in all

---

[10] Dawson, 38-39.
[11] F.C. Hsu, *Confucianism*. (Pondicherry, India: Sri Aurobindo International Centre of Education, 1966), 62-63.

human beings, and to which all things, including human beings owe their very existence.[12] Through the 'uncovering' and identification with this principle within oneself, as opposed to the simple adoption of it as a superficial outer behaviour, individuals could achieve harmony between 'Heaven and Earth' – both within themselves and as a fact in society. In relation to social and political structures it follows for Confucius that a society can achieve harmony only if it is led by a virtuous person. This leader, having developed the expression of Divine Love, sets the 'tone' or 'example' for cultural development and does nothing that would bring harm to the citizens. We see this as the consequence in a major principle espoused by Confucius:

> Tsze-Kung asked, saying, 'Is there one word which may serve as a rule of practice for all one's life?' The Master said, 'Is not Reciprocity such a word? What you do not want done to yourself, do not do to others.' (*Analect* 15:23)[13]

This rule of conduct, similar to the 'Golden Rule' in western doctrines, gives us some idea of both the activity of relationship between all members of society as well as the *activity of governance* instituted in this political system.

---

[12] Hsu, 63. F.C. Hsu describes it in this way: "Love is a mighty *vibration* coming straight from the One, and only the very pure and very strong are capable of receiving and manifesting it."

[13] James P. Sterba, *Social and Political Philosophy: Classical Western Texts in Feminist and Multicultural Perspectives.* (Wadsworth Publishing Company: Belmont, California. 1998), 46.

That is, the leader would require that no hardship be imposed on the citizens that they would not also accept upon themselves. This, in many respects, mirrors the "original position" stance discussed by Sterba in his chapter on Welfare Liberalism.[14] In that instance, the participants in the original position determine a set of basic-needs minimums to which *all* would be assured, thus, securing basic necessities for themselves regardless of the outcome of their position in society. In direct relation to Sterba's principle of a basic-needs minimum, we find this assertion made by Confucius:

> When a country is well governed, poverty and a mean condition are things to be ashamed of. When a country is ill governed, riches and honor are things to be ashamed of. (*Analect* 8:13)[15]

For Confucius, the presence of poverty in a wealthy society is the result of poor governance. Poor leadership, in turn, is the direct result of a leader lacking virtue. We can see this position in a clearer light if we consider the following statements put forward by Confucius:

> A disciple asked Confucius about government. Confucius said, 'See to it that there is enough food, enough arms, and the trust of the people in government.' (*Analect* 12:7)[16]

---

[14] Sterba, *Contemporary Social*, 12-19.
[15] Sterba, *Social and Political*, 43.
[16] Dawson, 111.

> The disciple asked, 'Since they have a large population, what is there to add?' Confucius said, 'Enrich them.' (*Analect* 13:9)[17]

The well-known Confucian scholar, Mencius, also appears to support the notion of basic-needs minimum for the citizens.

> At the same time I should also say it is wrong for a prince not to share his pleasures with his subjects. If you will find pleasure in your subject's pleasures, they will also find pleasure in yours. If you will sorrow with their sorrows, they will sorrow with yours. At no time has a man failed to become real king if he found pleasure with all the world and if he sorrowed with all the world.[18]

We see the natural role for the king was to ensure that the subjects, beginning with the most helpless, were able to enjoy the basic-needs required for survival. We see this idea repeated by Mencius throughout his conversations with various rulers:

> When the people have more grain, more fish, and turtles than they can eat, and more timber than they can use, then in the support of their parents when alive and in the mourning of them when dead, they will be able to have no regrets over

---

[17] Dawson, 65. Dawson qualifies *Analect* 13:9 with a further footnote on page 160: "Although Confucius thought a materialistic outlook on life to be petty and confusing, he nevertheless recognized the material element in social welfare and order."

[18] James R. Ware, *The Sayings of Mencius*. (New York: Mentor Books, 1960), 54.

anything left undone. This is the first step along the Kingly way.[19]

We can conclude, then, that the values promoted by Confucius, and supported by Mencius, recognized a basic-needs minimum for all members of society and particularly, as Mencius portrayed, for those less fortunate.[20]

The difference, however, that arises between this non-Western perspective and Sterba's conclusion is his assertion that a legitimate coercive institution is *necessary* to maintaining that basic-needs minimum. While it can be said that a State founded upon Confucian principles could certainly possess an army, it is important to understand its purpose and role in society. It appears true that Confucius was aware of the need to defend one's country against negative outside influences. However, it is also suggested in the Analects that he believed that the need for coercion against the citizenry reflected failed leadership and was not necessary in the presence of a virtuous leader. That is, correct rule and actions by the leader would lead to correct behaviour in the citizens. This can be noted if we look closely at the Analects.

> Chi K'ang asked Confucius about government. Confucius replied, 'To govern means to rectify. If you lead on the people with correctness, who will dare not be correct?' (*Analect* 12:17)[21]

---

[19] D. C. Lau, *Mencius*. (Harmondworth: Penguin Books, 1970), 51
[20] Ware, 56. In Book 1, Part B, Section 5, we see Mencius emphasizing that King Wen would always ensure the welfare of the lowest four classes first.
[21] Sterba, *Social and Political*, 44.

The need to develop a standard of truth in which the people can trust and be assured of appears to be part of establishing boundaries of correct behaviour for all. Rectification, or the need to recognise the truth of any circumstance in society and to deal with it in those terms, is a necessity in identifying what true needs are. This seems to be a major step toward eliminating the need for coercion – i.e. by modeling the virtuous behaviours upon which citizens would later adopt for their own behaviour. The result is clearly described for us further by Confucius.

> The Master said, 'When a prince's personal conduct is correct, his government is effective without the issuing of orders. If his personal conduct is not correct, he may issue orders, but they will not be followed.' (*Analect* 13:6)[22]

Confucius has distinctly pointed out the need for correct and virtuous behaviour by the leader. This becomes a powerful tool when combined with the previous notion of reciprocity. The leader establishes correct behaviour and then practices, through their governing principles, the idea of reciprocity. Confucius asserts that this influence on society would eventually eliminate the need for any form of coercive institution in society.

> The Master said, 'If good men were to govern a country in succession for a hundred years, they would be able to transform the violently bad, and

---

[22] Sterba, *Social and Political*, 45.

dispense with capital punishments.' (*Analect* 13:11)[23]

Like a parent who models good behaviour to inculcate responsibility and self-governance in their children it is the anchoring of virtue in a society, through the presence of a virtuous leader, that produces a responsible and self-governing citizenry. In western societies, this concept of modeling virtuous behaviours has been recognised as an imperative in raising children and instilling right relations but, curiously, remains entirely absent from any accepted model of political governance put forward or examined by Sterba. Whether he believes that virtuous behaviour is not possible or present in western political leadership or that the idea simply does not occur to him is not known. For western models of governance, systems providing a basic-needs minimum are only seen as sustainable through coercive actions against its citizenry. The need to "enforce orders" in the Confucian model is largely redundant and wholly contradictory as the members of society, from good governance, come to naturally develop the expression of their own innate ideal natures – namely, *jen.*

Philip J. Ivanhoe describes, in detail, the true sense of a Confucian society:

> In the well ordered state, society becomes the family, writ large. The king, as father to his people, must care for them and, as a proper parent, provide for them. The ruler must enrich his people – both materially and spiritually. The enlightened state is an extended family, providing

---

[23] Sterba, *Social and Political.* 45.

for the needs of all its members while preserving a strict hierarchy in its structure. Most important of all, the enlightened state, like the ideal family, is permeated at every level with a deep concern for each of its members.

The moral life is the life lived cultivating oneself for participation in this enlightened state. But the commitment is never one of *enlightened self-interest*; participation in such a society affords one the unique opportunity of fulfilling one's *destiny* as a human being. The relationships one enters into as a member of society are not restrictive; they are liberating and fulfilling.[24]

In this humane form of society, the need for coercive institutions could be, as Confucius asserts, eliminated entirely and permanently in less than a century. The presence of *jen* in all facets of social and private life serves to limit the military's function to external conflicts and defence of the nation. It is obvious that Sterba has failed to consider what effects virtuous governance might have on a nation and its people. His western bias toward strictly coercive forms of governance incorrectly maintains that any form of social justice can only be sustained through enforcement by institutions.

We have seen, then, how Confucian ideology supports the standard of a basic-needs minimum in society and that it can be realised without the needs for permanent coercive institutions. Sterba's justification for permanent coercive institutions to enforce those standards does not stand as an absolute. Relative to the Confucian

---

[24] Philip J. Ivanhoe, *Ethics in the Confucian Tradition*. (Atlanta: Scholars Press, 1990), 6-7.

ideal, abandonment of this benevolent approach in later systems of governance, up to and including the present, would speak to one of the primary difficulties encountered in establishing social and political systems absent of the need for coercive institutions. Confucian philosophy would deny the need for permanent coercive institutions by recognising that the expressions of *jen*, *reciprocity* and *rectification* in the governance of the State would eventually and necessarily lead to harmonious social systems. Western governments, on the other hand, issue laws for its citizens under the threat of coercion and penalty in hopes that this imposed order will produce harmony. As a result, their approach *demands* coercive institutions in order to be maintained.[25] In light of Confucian thought, such coercive institutions are anathema to creating a harmonious society and a general resentment of the government and dishonesty in the citizenry would be the result.

Sterba aptly recognises the opportunity in investigating non-western cultures in that, "sometimes, as in the case of American Indian culture, there will be important lessons to learn."[26] In the case of Confucian philosophy, we can see just how valuable these lessons might be and that the traditional exclusion of non-western

---

[25] Ivanhoe, 6-7.

[26] What the reader may have realized at this point is that the values espoused in Confucian philosophy are similarly present in other western traditions such as in the virtues expressed in Christianity, Islam and Judaism, and through western philosophers such as is found in Plato's *Republic*. As these ideals seem yet untried in the history of western civilisation is all the more pitiful for western society.

perspectives in western educational institutions may turn out to be more costly than expected. Indeed, the cost may come in the failure of western governments and societies to recognise and uphold essential human qualities leading to the collapse of their social, political and economic systems.

Nondualism and Bridging the Gaps in International Development

> Without sharing there can be no justice.
> Without justice there can be no peace.
> Without peace there can be no future.
> —*Maitreya, the World Teacher*

The discrepancy between the 'nature of reality' and our 'perceptions of that reality' has been the topic of debate in philosophical, religious and scientific circles for thousands of years. From the delineations of Pythagoras and Plato to the illuminations of Aquinas or Rumi, our understanding of metaphysical reality has been enhanced and enriched by a wealth of perspectives. More recently, investigators in the field of quantum physics have given us a glimpse behind the veil of material reality and shown the world a landscape surprisingly similar to that celebrated throughout millennia by countless mystics. What appears to us as a material world, inhabited by a multiplicity of distinct and autonomous beings, is no less than the outer garment of an energetic universe that is substantially nondual, unified and whole. Our sensory perceptions are responsible for this seemingly pluralistic façade and fashion a veneer of separateness that disassociates and disconnects our awareness from the nondual ground of our being. This split between appearance and reality – or more properly, between epistemology and ontology – has challenged thinkers for untold centuries and is one of the central factors influencing the way individuals and societies have related to one another.

These relationships naturally extend between the have and have-not societies and approaches to social and economic development reveal a great deal about underlying attitudes and perspectives. Indeed, the very existence of these two extremes in society suggests a deeper disharmony in the way we understand our place in the world. The split between appearance and reality can often be one of the central factors motivating our response to the development needs of others whose beneficent outcome can be measured in terms of *justice*. Where the approach has been grounded in the dualist perspective, development has tended to focus largely on outer economic and material needs to the detriment of human dignity and equality.

Alternatively, nondual perspectives have traditionally nurtured a sensed interdependence and deeper identification with the needs of others. Development which has been influenced by this impetus has emphasised the creation of conditions that nourish community, culture and creativity. This raises some important questions with regard to the ways in which dualism and nondualism influence and affect our approach to international development. Does our conditioned perception of individual material autonomy promote a fundamental separativeness in our relationships and does that perceptual illusion impact negatively on our efforts to manifest justice in social and economic relations? I suggest that it does and that this basic misunderstanding has had a profoundly negative impact on justice within our approaches to global development and the alleviation of poverty.

The dichotomy and contradiction arising out of the simultaneous existence of a dualistic epistemology (the way we see the world) and nondualistic ontology (actual reality) constitutes *the* spiritual crisis for humanity today. What amounts to a true paradigm shift for humanity at this time, nondualism not only threatens to upset the status quo of the hyper-individualism lying back of the current global economic order but offers a unifying approach to life that validates the deepest intuitions of our spiritual nature. Therefore, it is imperative to examine ways in which this perspective of unity and interconnectedness can provide a new blueprint for social progress based in cooperation, justice and sharing.

Seeing Is Believing: taking dualism at face value

It is not my intention to forward a rejection of dualism. Rather, it is important to recognise the illusion that dualism generates and to find a proper place for the dualistic perspective in our approach to life. The subject-object perspective of dualism constitutes the means by which we interact with the world around us and is critical for engaging with the mundane aspects of our material world. However, this perspective cannot, and should not, be coherently extended to questions of meaning, purpose or ontology. A statement such as this has enormous implications. Understanding the reasons behind this is central to developing strategies based in nondualist philosophy.

The basic underlying position in this essay is that human beings suffer a great illusion of *separation.* Fundamentally speaking, we believe ourselves to be autonomous and separate from one another, resulting in actions and an approach to life which causes enormous suffering. This illusion of separation has also led to a dangerously unbalanced response to conditions in the world. Our external sensory perceptions convey to us a wealth of information about the physical universe and provide us with a centralised and autonomous orientation to the world. As life unfolds before us we perceive ourselves as distinct material subjects in a world of external material objects and this separative dualistic perception provides the foundation upon which we develop our personal identity and relationships. A variety of strategies and responses are cultivated in order to relate to the world from this subject-object perspective and this point of view becomes deeply embedded within our psyche. It provides the psychological constraints within which we make most of our determinations about the nature of ourselves and our relationship to others in the world. One could reasonably claim that much of our personal identity and routines in life are, in fact, derived from that dualistic mental scaffolding. For many, "seeing is believing" and the immediacy of our persisting sensory experiences continually reinforce the rigid conception of a fragmented material universe.

Dualistic conditioning is further complicated by the fact that language, itself a mode of communication between two seemingly distinct and separate entities, is fundamentally grounded in subject-object relations. As a result, it is difficult to even discuss nondual perspectives without clothing those discussions in the dualistic terminology present in most languages. The overwhelming strength of the dualistic perspective is in its power to arrest and imprison our attention. Nondualist perspectives require a persistent effort at delving behind the veil of appearances. According to Alfred North Whitehead, we observe the world around us as a subject amongst objects and, going forward with only this data, we otherwise assume that we have acquired a *complete* set of details regarding the components of our experience.[1] The thoroughness of our knowledge, therefore, is only as complete as our observations – which in themselves do not include the greater components of a nondual reality. In other words, we observe the world in dualistic terms and where we can't directly observe – that is, when thinking about such as notions as consciousness, ontology, teleology or God – we fill in the blanks with dualistic conceptions. The unfortunate conclusion for this perceptual feedback loop is that *appearance is equal to reality*. Whitehead has illustrated the danger of relying upon material appearances in making determinations about the nature of reality and our relationship with it, and it is this fundamental error in perception that now threatens our economic and social development.

The notion of separateness, a fundamental characteristic of the dualist perspective, comes from the Latin root *separatus*, meaning "to pull apart." Some western scholars and theologians,

---

[1] Alfred North Whitehead, *Process and Reality*. Corrected edition. (New York: The Free Press, 1978), 4.

such as Swedenborg and Schleiermacher,[2] have suggested that the biblical story of humanity's fall from paradise in the Garden of Eden is essentially the story of the origins of a *perceptual* or *psychological* separation from the divinity within the human being. More specifically, a perceptual break or revolution from an original nondual spiritual unity to later materialistic self-perception provided the backdrop for humanity's self-imposed exile from its earlier identification with the Divine. This historical contraction of individual human identity would constitute what many might argue is *the* original sin for humanity. The edifice of self-distinction, which we refer to as our individualized identity, is not only integral in revealing the existence of a *personal* will but it is also logically responsible for much of what has so far been experienced

---

[2] According to the philosopher and scientist Emanuel Swedenborg, human consciousness is uniquely equipped to experience Reality in two ways: as the original state of divine Oneness with God; or as witnessing a separate self-existence, enchanted by the sensory appeal of its field of experience. Humanity's return to God involves a free will choice between the world of appearances and the underlying reality of our essential Oneness with God. In the Creation myth this is represented as the choice between eating from the Tree of Knowledge or from the Tree of Life.

Later, the philosopher and theologian Friedrich Schleiermacher built on the notion of a "fall" from an originally unified identity with God, or God consciousness, to a subsequent separate (and separative) self-consciousness. It is through this descent into material existence that our awareness of the infinite fragments, resulting in the experience of partition from God.

negatively within the individual as a result of the misuse of that will. Considering the wide assortment of negative emotions accessible to the human being, it is impossible to imagine the existence of such conditions as jealousy, greed, doubt, fear, loneliness, criticism or resentment without there first possessing that individual conviction of separateness. I am not here presenting any ultimate judgement about personal will other than to identify that it arises alongside the development of the separate individual identity. As to whether this is good or bad is yet to be demonstrated by humanity and whether we can eventually employ that will in the context of being part of the Whole, and to the benefit of the Whole of which we are part.

Therefore, the "original sin" as the illusion of separateness lies behind much of human pain, suffering and misery experienced by mankind. Re-awakening to nondual reality represents a restoration of that unified relationship to the Divine, with a consequent approach to relationship based in unity, love and brotherhood. These are significant claims and warrant serious reflection. They are also inevitable expressions where a nondual unity is known to be a factual foundation of reality.

The Dichotomy: nondualism, to dualism, and back again

Albert Einstein once declared that everything was energy in some form or another. Our senses capture fragmented snapshots from our perceptions of this energetic ocean and weave these together in a cinematic mosaic of material activity. Within that mosaic we construct identity based upon those perceived orientations within that space. More recently, quantum physicists have expanded upon this view of nondual reality and many aspects of this emerging perspective appear to be as much at home in the Sufic pantheism of Ibn Al-Arabi, or the Emptiness discourses by the Buddhist philosopher Nāgārjuna, as they do in contemporary scientific journals. New evidence demands that we now re-examine the nature and purpose of our being and actions.

The study of consciousness, spirituality and the human mind has been taken up by a new set of investigators – notably, modern-day physicists and philosophers. This unlikely group of 'psychoanalysts' has made strange bedfellows with the more traditional investigators. New insights through quantum physics have upset our picture of the universe in ways that can be difficult to grasp and require a fundamental shift in our traditional ontological views. An experiment by Alain Aspect in 1982 demonstrated a basic principle in quantum physics known as *non-locality*. Aspect provided evidence of what can only be described by physicists as a *transcendent* non-material level of reality called the *non-local* domain through which information could pass from one material object to another beyond the restrictions of time and space.[3] This signal-less transmission of information could occur instantaneously (faster than the speed of light) regard-less of position or location in the space and demonstrates the existence of a field

---

[3] Alain Aspect; J. Dalibard; and G. Roger, "Experimental Test of Bell Inequalities Using Time-Varying Analyzers." *Physical Review Letters 49*, 1982, 1804.

of interconnectivity known previously only to mystics and seers. Concepts such as non-locality undermine the conclusions of our sensory perceptions and challenge our self-conceptions as separate material beings. It also assures us of an existence far more integral and unified than what is merely witnessed as the physical world. Quantum physics recognises the non-local domain as the realm where the physical 'subject-object' world lies in potential, awaiting manifestation. This omniscient, omnipresent, energetic state is transformed into an observable material 'particle-state' through a process called the *collapse of the wave function* and it is here where the interplay of consciousness becomes paramount.

Quantum theory opens a new line of thinking regarding the causal powers of consciousness. Rather than merely an instrument of awareness, consciousness must now be ascribed causal powers, forcing us to radically change our understanding about consciousness itself. This new awareness necessitates that consciousness be a universal property, *sub-atomically* present in the field of each mathematical point in space, and not simply 'localised' to individual subjects as *we* experience it.[4]

---

[4] I chose the word *experience* to indicate consciousness in a global sense. However, there are many definitions and gradations that would confine this feature strictly to humans. Consciousness, in the way employed here, does not require the ability to under-stand or analyse experiences, only that experience occurs and elicits a coherent and ordered response; psychologically, emotionally or physically. In this sense, even an atom can be said to be conscious.

A simple way of understanding this is to say that consciousness exits universally, as one unified field, but is experienced individually as a personal attribute. All human beings have consciousness, yet experience it as distinct, separate and autonomous. This is significant because it directly demonstrates the unified interconnection and interdependence at the quantum level of reality. It also frees consciousness from being a possession solely of individuals. Notions suggesting that consciousness is limited to the confines of the human brain are no longer defensible. Quantum physics suggests that something more fundamental and spiritual is in place for the human being.

Dr. Larry Dossey, former Chief of Staff of Medical City Dallas Hospital, draws attention to the overwhelming evidence that 'mind' behaves in a non-local way. As a consequence, "if mind is non-local, [then] there is one mind, or Universal Mind."[5] Dossey suggests that this Universal Mind possesses all the characteristics of "what the West has regarded as Soul" [6] and that current scientific evidence is asking us to consider that human beings are an integral manifestation and expression of that Consciousness. Menos Kafatos and Robert Nadeau looked at the implications this has for humanity: "If one can accept this argument [that the universe is a conscious Whole], then the profound sense of alienation that has seemingly been occasioned by the success of classical [dualistic] physics from the

---

[5] Betsy Whitfill, "Recovering the Soul: An Interview with Dr. Larry Dossey" *Share International.* Vol. 10, No. 7, September 1991, 13.
[6] Whitfill, 13.

eighteen century to the present could be rather dramatically alleviated."⁷ Indeed, the expanding *global* awareness of our essential unity is nothing short of revolutionary.

This perspective compels us to consider an entirely new approach to life. Amit Goswami, professor of physics in the Institute of Theoretical Sciences at the University of Oregon, agrees with this view and reminds adherents of the particle-based perspective of the universe that this new philosophical viewpoint "does not say that matter is unreal, but that the reality of matter is secondary to that of consciousness, which is *itself* the ground of all being – including matter."⁸ Goswami explains that the human mind consists of both a *quantum* and *classical* component of the brain-mind. The *quantum* component, he writes, is "regenerative and its states are multifaceted. It is the vehicle for conscious choice and for creativity."⁹ This facet of the mind allows us to experience fleeting moments of the quantum unity-consciousness and it aids in the comprehension of experiences that would be unavailable to us in a strictly material universe. Such experiences include intuition, dêja vu, ESP, telekinesis, telepathy, or near-death-experiences. In essence, the *quantum* component allows us to register aspects of our universal and interdependent nature.

---

⁷ Menas Kafatos and Robert Nadeau, *The Conscious Universe: Part and Whole in Modern Physical Theory.* (New York: Springer-Verlag New York, Inc., 1990), 10.
⁸ Amit Goswami, *The Self-Aware Universe: how consciousness creates the material* world. (New York: Putnam, 1993), 10-11.
⁹ Goswami, 162.

Alternately, the *classical* component represents the concrete aspect of mind that registers sensory perceptions and stores sensory data, thoughts and memories. These features act as a reference point for material experience and the formation of a coherent 'self-identity' occurs in this region of the brain-mind, assembled from the perceived subject-object relations.[10] As Goswami explains, individuals function with a fragment of that underlying Consciousness, which has conveniently formed an individual identity as a 'localized point of reference' in the material world. Being energetic in nature, this thought-form of 'self' becomes the actual barrier to subsequent experiences of its own essential vast nature. The strength of this barrier, it follows, exists relative to the intensity and conviction by which that thought-form is held in place. The more separate one becomes through rigid identifications and beliefs, the more disconnected one becomes from experiencing the nondual nature of quantum reality. A painful paradox becomes evident: *the more we attempt to create a real and substantive identity in the world the more disconnected and alienated we become from that world.* Moreover, it is the drive to develop current day hyper-individualism, along with the attendant qualities associated with that (such as greed, competitiveness, selfishness and alienation) which is also driving our failures to solve the problems of hunger, war, poverty and suffering in the world. The drive to exist as distinct and separate material beings conditions the way in which consciousness continues to maintain the psychological barrier of identity

---

[10] Goswami, 162.

between the individual and the cosmos. Through their response to dualistic perceptions of the world, individuals repeat that earlier expulsion from Eden. Where consciousness can free itself from this psychological conditioning so, too, will it begin to experience aspects of universality and a deeper affinity with nature and with each other. One must lose the 'self' to find the Self. This has been taught for ages and could, once again, bring deeper meaning to our struggles in the world.

Dualism: sowing the seeds of separation

We have seen how dualistic perceptions of the world create a powerful illusion for identity. This illusion fragments experience and obstructs awareness of the underlying universal unity. The result is a growing deficiency in the ability to identify with others and an increasing disconnection from the inner source of *livingness*. Consequently, the more successful we become in projecting our identity onto the outer material world the more we experience a disconnection from the world and others. In that alienated condition we diminish our ability for compassion and the result of this, obviously, will have a devastating toll on our interactions with the world.

The term *compassion* comes from the Latin roots *passio*, meaning "to suffer"; and *cum*, meaning "together with". Compassion, as the ability to suffer together with another, is a manifestation of our fundamental interconnection and identification with others. *Social and economic development is a manifestation of compassion, and those efforts in global development demonstrate justice only insofar as they serve needs that are identified through compassion.* A nondual worldview is the reality by which we are able to infuse our actions with justice. It is also the means by which we fulfill our essential spiritual nature.

Current strategies in third world development often represent a complex combination of perspectives alternating variously between the dichotomies of dualism and nondualism. In social and economic development, the dichotomy of dualist versus nondualist perspectives can traditionally be seen working out in interesting and diverse ways. Dualist perspectives have often approached development in a more conservative-minded fashion – focusing largely on the outer material conditions through which human beings might develop or enhance their own material wellbeing without seeing oneself as involved or responsible for that wellbeing. This approach emphasises improvements in the outer economic conditions that will lead to material prosperity and expression as autonomous material beings. Economic development is typically viewed as the primary vehicle for that individual expression. Unfortunately, attempts to consolidate and substantiate that autonomy more than often sow the seeds of separation that lead to further alienation and disconnection.

While there are many examples of dualistic approaches to development, Structural Adjustment Programs (SAPs) promoted by the IMF and World Bank over the last three decades will suffice to offer one of the clearest examples of attempts to increase material prosperity as a means to improve human welfare. These programs often fail to appreciate the essential interdependence between the impoverished and their environment, and foreign corporations are often given unfettered access to local markets and public resources in exchange for development loans. By increasing levels of competition and material inequity at the lowest levels of society these programs have demonstrated a failure to identify with the fundamental interdependent needs of humans and their societies. In an article to the *Economist* in 1999, Tony Clarke spoke of the devastating effect that this approach has had on developing nations.

> Structural adjustment programmes imposed by the World Bank since the 1980s in exchange for debt relief has made it easier for TNCs [transnational corporations] to manufacture products for export, extract valuable natural resources, obtain generous investment incentives, take advantage of cheap labour conditions, redirect local production priorities, and endlessly repatriate profits, unfettered by government intervention or regulation.[11]

Attempts to instil humanity and compassion to these programs are often met with resistance in a form that places material economic priorities over human welfare. Yet it is clear that these divisive policies are unsustainable as long-term strategies for global development. In its analysis on global development, the Meltzer Report stated in 2000 that "the World Bank is irrelevant rather than central to the goal of eliminating global

---

[11] Tony Clarke, "Twilight of the Corporation", *The Ecologist*, 29, 2. May/June, 1999, 158.

poverty"[12] and even the World Bank itself has indicated that its attempt to realize a positive development impact had a failure rate of 65-70% in the poorest countries.[13] Why should such a collection of intelligently derived protocols for development yield such continuously devastating results in circumstance after circumstance? In his 1998 work *The Grip of Death*, Michael Rowbotham describes the damaging effects that some of these programs have wreaked on the Third World.

> Between 1980 and 1989 some thirty-three African countries received 241 structural adjustment loans. During that same period, average GDP per capita in those countries fell 1.1% p. a., whilst per capita food production also experienced steady decline. The real value of the minimum wage dropped by over 25%, government expenditure on education fell from $11 billion to $7 billion and primary school enrollments dropped from 80% in 1980 to 69% in 1990. The number of poor people in these countries rose from 184 million in 1985 to 216 million in 1990, an increase of 17%." In *Goodbye America*, he stressed that "no Third World country that has borrowed from the World Bank has subsequently found its way out of debt.[14]

Adam Smith, in *The Wealth of Nations*, was clear in asserting that infant economies required protection in order to achieve sustainability. The

---

[12] Walden Bello, "Meltzer Report on Bretton Woods Twins Builds Case for Abolition but Hesitates", *Focus on Trade* 48, April 2000.
[13] Bello.
[14] Rowbotham, Michael. *The Grip of Death.* (London: Jon Carpenter Publishing, 1998).

inherent logic in his position recognised the need for economies to serve the interests of local communities rather than the inverse. Edward Herman, professor of finances at Wharton School at the University of Pennsylvania, reiterated this point in his article *The Threat of Globalisation*.

> ...no country, past or present, has taken off into sustained economic growth and moved from economic backwardness to modernity without large-scale government protection and subsidization of infant industries and other modes of insulation from domination by powerful outsiders. This includes Great Britain, the United States, Japan, Germany, South Korea and Taiwan, all highly protectionist in the earlier takeoff phases of their growth process."[15]

The period wherein entry into the global economy is undertaken marks a period where nondualist principles must overwhelmingly apply. It is a period where the survival of that economy depends fully upon the ability of others in the market to express compassion and where emphasis is placed on securing the fundamental security and sustainability of the emerging community. In a challenge to the economic policies that placed economies above communities, E. F. Schumacher wrote in *Small is Beautiful* that,

> A modern economist may engage in highly sophisticated calculations on whether full employment 'pays' or whether it might be more 'economic' to run an economy on less than full

---

[15] Edward S. Herman, "The Threat of Globalisation", *Economic Reform Australia*, Newsletter, 2nd Dec., 1999.

employment so as to ensure a greater mobility of labour, a better stability of wages, and so forth...this is standing the truth on its head by considering goods as more important than people and consumption as more important than creative activity.[16]

Emphasis upon the development of material prosperity without an understanding of that prosperity as a means toward human dignity often results in policies that lack the essential elements of justice. Programs based solely in terms of economic advantage usually lack the conditions needed to sustain communal and familial relations, and economics without compassion interprets human labour as a capital expenditure that suffocates economic expansion. As a result, human beings become liabilities within the very systems intended to sustain them.

In such an environment, lack of compassion can have a devastating effect on developing nations resulting in enormous injustices. Third world development has become a lucrative business for rich nations. As Edward Goldsmith writes in his assessment of the present global situation, "The aim of 'development' is not to improve the lives of Third World citizens, but to ensure a market for Western goods and services, and a source of cheap labour and raw materials for big corporations. Global development is

---

[16] E. F. Schumacher, *Small is Beautiful: A Study Of Economics As If People Mattered*. (London: Abacus, 1973), 46-7.

imperialism without the need for military conquest."[17]

Recent figures from the World Bank indicated that in 1998 the 41 HIPC (Heavily Indebted Poor Countries) transferred $1.68 billion more to the northern industrialised nations than they received. This figure is nearly equal to the average annual amounts transferred by the US to Europe under the Marshall Plan between 1947 and 1953. The main difference in the present global situation, however, is that the poorest nations of the South – already ravaged by war, government corruption, drought, widespread poverty and disease, and economic collapse – are the unwilling investors funding the massive capital ventures of those highly advanced industrialised nations in the North. When witnessed from this perspective one must question how we have become so disconnected from our fellow human beings that we could completely fail to identify with their suffering. It is clear from this point alone that if we are to make real headway in human and social development we will necessarily have to ground our development programs in nondualist considerations.

Nondualism: bridging the gaps in development

A nondualist perspective views the world as an integrated whole infused with the potency of consciousness in every atom. All life is seen as an integral expression of that underlying unity –

---

[17] Edward Goldsmith, "Empires without armies", *The Ecologist*, 29. 2. May/June 1999, 154.

requiring only the societal frameworks necessary to bring that spiritual potential to manifestation. Actions grounded in a nondualist metaphysic consider the interconnection and interdependence of all things and a failure to restore justice in one area of the world is a failure of justice in the global society as a whole. Such considerations place an imperative upon working cooperatively to restore balance and harmony in our global relationships and, relative to the diversity we witness in the world, it also suggests the need to appreciate unique ways in which different societies manifest human potential.

Nondualist perspectives have historically demonstrated a more liberal approach by emphasising social and economic development as a way of maximizing human growth and potential. Because a higher value is placed on the interior experience of human interdependence and interconnection, efforts would tend to focus on directly enhancing the individual's inner life and development. According to the Commission on Global Governance, co-chaired by former Swedish Prime Minister Ingvar Carlsson and former Secretary-General of the Commonwealth Shridath Ramphal, there is simply "no alternative to working together."[18] In identifying the rapid changes facing humanity at this time, the Global Governance commission tried to emphasise the necessity of developing new perspectives for understanding global neighbourhood and underscored the unavoidable

---

[18] *Our Global Neighbourhood: The Report of The Commission on Global Governance.* (Oxford: Oxford University Press, 1995), 2.

obligation to work from a perspective of interdependence.

Today's interdependencies are compelling people to recognise the unity of the world. People are forced not just to be neighbours but to be good neighbours. The practical needs of a shared habitat and the instinct of human solidarity are pointing in the same direction. More than ever before, people need each other—for their welfare, their health, their safety, perhaps even for their survival.[19]

There have been several programs and declarations put forward over the last century to express these principles of unity and which sought to advance human circumstances on the notions of compassion, justice, global interdependence and human dignity. A few examples of these include the Marshall Plan (1947), the United Nations Universal Declaration of Human Rights (1948), the Commission on International Development (1969), the Commission on Global Governance (1995), Jubilee 2000 (2000) and the Millennium Development Goals (2000). However, one plan remains far and above the most comprehensive concrete strategy toward the expression of global unity and interdependence than any other.

In 1980, the former chancellor of West Germany, Willy Brandt, chaired the Independent Commission on International Development Issues (ICIDI). Brandt's panel of former world leaders and prominent figures examined the existing state of global economic injustice wherein developing nations of the South

---

[19] *Global Neighbourhood*, 349.

remained largely arrested and socially enslaved to the dominant economic influences of the industrialised North. The commission published their findings in a report called *North-South: A Programme for Survival* that provided a blueprint for global economic renewal based in the view that humanity was one interdependent family necessitating a system of global economic cooperation. The divisions that infected relations between the industrialised North and the developing South were identified as the key challenges to overcome and a failure to do so promised fatal consequences for the global community. In representing the convictions of the commission, Brandt wrote that the two decades leading up to the millennium were critical for mankind and that "many global issues will come to a head during this period."[20] More than at any other time, he explained, "the focus has to be not on machines or institutions but on people."[21] The commission clearly recognised the need to prioritise development as a function of compassion, human dignity and justice rather than economy. Economics was identified as the central arena through which this renewal could be implemented as a means to long-term global security.

Recognising the rapid deterioration of the world situation and the rising tension between the global 'have' and 'have-nots' the commission recommended the implementation of a short-

---

[20] *North-South: A Program for Survival.* Report of the Independent Commission on International Development Issues under the Chairmanship of Willy Brandt. (Cambridge: MIT Press, 1980), 7.
[21] *North-South*, 23.

term emergency program to end poverty in developing nations. Simultaneously, a new round of global negotiations leading to a full-scale restructuring of the global economy along the lines of cooperation, justice and sharing of the world's resources would secure the long-term prosperity and security for all nations. The commission expressed the fervent belief that "the present predicament of the world economy can be resolved only with a major international effort for the linking of resources to developmental needs, on the one hand, and the full utilization of under-utilized capacities on the other."[22]

The Brandt Report was presented by Willy Brandt to United Nations Secretary-General Kurt Waldheim on February 12, 1980. Ambassadors from more than one hundred nations endorsed the Brandt Report in their opening statements at the UN General Assembly in September 1980 and again in September 1981. To date, the report remains the only comprehensive blueprint for global reform to have received international consensus and, in terms of long-term security and stability, remains one of the few approaches to global development and endorsed by the United Nations that can begin to manifest the principles of nonduality. The Commission on Global Governance intelligently recognised the critical nature of the present time and the urgent need to move beyond traditional development efforts.

> We are prompted to recall the vision that drove the process of founding the United Nations and the spirit of innovation that ushered in a new era

---

[22] *North-South*, 254.

of global governance. We need that spirit again today, together with a readiness to look beyond the United Nations and nation-states to the new forces that can now contribute to improved governance in the global neighbourhood. We fear that if reform is left to normal processes, only piecemeal and inadequate action will result. We look, therefore, to a more deliberate process.[23]

The Brandt plan was such a deliberate process and a new sense of urgency surrounding global justice must now counteract our complacency. Our global neighbourhood is on fire and this crisis demands the most urgent response grounded in compassion. At no other time in human history has such a horrendous injustice assailed our fellow brothers and sisters, and we have arrived at a period where compassion between individuals must now be extended across nations. Through nondualism and a unified vision of humanity we can reconnect to our humanity and our compassion to ensure justice and dignity for all.

---

[23] *Global Neighbourhood*, 350.

Bibliography

Al-Arabi, Muhyiddin Ibn. *The Seals Of Wisdom: From The Fusus Al-Hakim.* ed. Raghavan Iyer. London: Concord Grove Press, 1983.

Albert, David Z. *Quantum Mechanics and Experience.* Harvard University Press: Cambridge, 1992.

Anacker, Stefan. *Seven Works of Vasubandhu: The Buddhist Psychological Doctor.* Delhi: Motilal Banarsidass Publishers, 1984.

Angeles, Peter A. *Dictionary of Philosophy.* Barnes & Noble Books: New York, 1981.

Arberry, A. J. *Sufism.* New York: Harper Torchbooks, 1970.

Aspect, A.; Dalibard, J.; and Roger, G. "Experimental Test of Bell Inequalities Using Time-Varying Analyzers." *Physical Review Letters.* 49, 1982.

Bello, W. "Meltzer Report on Bretton Woods Twins Builds Case for Abolition but Hesitates", *Focus on Trade.* 48, April 2000.

Benveniste, Émile. "Subjectivity in Language" *Critical Theory Since 1965.* Edited by Hazard Adams and Leroy Searle. Gainesville: University Presses of Florida, 1986. 728-732.

Berliant, Arnold. "The Aesthetics of Art and Nature." *Landscape, Natural Beauty and the Arts.* Edited by Salim Kemal and Ivan Gaskell. New York: Cambridge University Press, 1993.

Bohm, David. *Wholeness and the Implicate Order.* London: Routledge & Kegan Paul, 1980.

Bradley, F. H. *Appearance and Reality*. Oxford: Oxford University Press, 1978.

Capra, Fritjof. *The Tao of Physics: An Exploration of the Parallels Between Modern Physics and Eastern Mysticism*. London: HarperCollins Publishers, 1982.

Carlson, Allan. *The Aesthetics of Nature: An Introduction*. (pre-publication). p. 9-10.

Carlson, Allen. "Appreciation and the Natural Environment," *The Journal of Aesthetics and Art Criticism*. XXXVII 3, Spring 1979.

Clarke, T. "Twilight of the Corporation", *The Ecologist*. 29, 2. May/June, 1999.

Conze, Edward. *Buddhism: Its Essence and Development*. New York: Harper Torchbooks, 1959.

Davis, Paul. *God and the New Physics*. New York: Simon & Shuster, 1983.

Dawson, Raymond. *Confucius*. London, England: Oxford University Press, 1981.

Dennett, Daniel C. *Darwin's Dangerous Idea*. New York: Touchstone, 1995.

Denny, Frederick Mathewson. *An Introduction to Islam*. New York: Macmillan Publishing Company, 1994.

Dhammapada. translated by Juan Mascaró. London: Penguin Books, 1973.

Eliade, Mircea. *Shamanism: Archaic Techniques of Ecstasy*. Translated by Willard R. Trask. Princeton: Princeton University Press, 1964.

Goswami, Amit. *The Self-Aware Universe: How Consciousness Creates the Material World.* Tarcher/Putnam: New York, 1993.

Goldsmith, E. "Empires without armies", *The Ecologist.* 29. 2. May/June,1999.

Grim, John A. *The Shaman: Patterns of Siberian and Ojibway Healing.* Norman: University of Oklahoma Press, 1983.

Habermas, Jürgen. *Knowledge and Human Interests.* Boston: Beacon Press, 1968.

Hegel, Georg Wilhelm Friedrich. *Phenomenology of Spirit.* Translated by A. V. Miller. Oxford: Oxford University Press, 1977.

Hepbur, R. W. "Contemporary Aesthetics and the Neglect of Natural Beauty", *British Analytical Philosophy.* Edited by Bernard Williams and Alan Montefore. (Routledge and Kegan Paul Ltd.: London, 1996). p. 289-290.

Herbert, Nick. *Elemental Mind: Human Consciousness and the New Physics.* New York: Penguin Books,1993.

Herman, E. S. "The Threat of Globalisation", *Economic Reform Australia Newsletter.* 2nd Dec., 1999.

History of Philosophy Eastern and Western, Vol. II. Edited by Sarvepalli Radhakrishnan. Unwin Brothers Limited: London, 1953.

Hobbes, Thomas. *Leviathan.* Cambridge: Cambridge University Press, 1997.

Hsu, F.C. *Confucianism.* Pondicherry, India: Sri Aurobindo International Centre of Education, 1966.

Husaini, S.A.Q. *The Pantheistic Monism of Ibn Al-Arabi.* Lahore: Ashraf Press, 1970.

Ivanhoe, Philip J. *Ethics in the Confucian Tradition.* Atlanta: Scholars Press, 1990.

Jung, C. G. *Synchronicity: An Acausal Connecting Principle.* Princeton: Princeton University Press, 1973.

Kafatos, Menas and Nadeau, Robert. *The Conscious Universe: Part and Whole in Modern Physical Theory.* New York: Springer-Verlag, 1990.

Jilek, Wolfgang G. *Indian Healing: Shamanic Ceremonialism in the Pacific Northwest Today.* Surry: Hancock House Publishers, Ltd., 1982.

Kafatos, M. and Nadeau, R. *The Conscious Universe: Part and Whole in Modern Physical Theory.* New York: Springer-Verlag New York, Inc., 1990.

Kalupahana, David J. *Mulamadhyamakarika of Nagarjuna: The Philosophy of the Middle Way.* Delhi: Motilal Banarsidass Publishers, 1986.

King-Farlow, John. *Self-Knowledge and Social Relations.* Science History Publications: New York, 1978.

Kinsley, David R., *Hinduism: A Cultural Perspective.* Englewood Cliffs: Prentice Hall, 1993.

Lacan, Jacques. "The Agency of the Letter in the Unconscious or Reason Since Freud" *Critical Theory Since 1965.* Edited by Hazard Adams and Leroy Searle. Gainesville: University Presses of Florida, 1986. 738-753.

Lata, Prem. *Mystic Saints of India: Shri Ramana Maharshi.* New Delhi: Sumit Publications, 1986.

Lau, D. C. *Mencius.* Harmondworth: Penguin Books, 1970.

Loy, David. *Nonduality: A Study of Comparative Philosophy.* New York: Humanity Books, 1998.

Mascaro, Juan. *The Upanishads.* London: Penguin Books, 1965.

Mindell, Arnold. *Quantum Mind: The Edge Between Physics and Psychology.* Portland: Lao Tse Press, 2000.

Müller, Max. ed., *Sacred Books of the East Series: The Upanishads, Part II.* trans. By Max Müller. Delhi: Motilal Banarsidass, 1965.

Nicholson, Reynold A. *Rumi: Poet and Mystic (1207-1273: Selections from His Writings).* London: Allen & Unwin, 1950.

North-South: A Programme for Survival. Cambridge: MIT Press, 1980.

Osborne, Arthur. *Ramana Maharshi and the Path of Self-Knowledge.* London: Rider and Company, 1970.

Our Global Neighbourhood: The Report of The Commission on Global Governance. Oxford: Oxford University Press, 1995.

Outwaite, William. *Habermas: A Critical Introduction.* Stanford: Stanford University Press, 1994.

Plato. *Republic.* translated by Richard W. Sterling and William C. Scott. W. W. Norton and Company: New York, 1985.

Bibliography

Rawls, John A. *A Theory of Justice*. Cambridge: Harvard University Press, 1971.

Rogers, Spence L. *The Shaman's Healing Way*. Ramona: Acoma Books, 1976.

_____. *The Shaman: His Symbols and His Healing Power*. Springfield: Charles C. Thomas Publishers, 1982.

Rowbotham, Michael. *The Grip of Death*. London: Jon Carpenter Publishing, 1998.

Russell, Bertrand. *Logical Atomism*. Unwin Brothers Limited: London, 1956.

Samuel, Geoffrey. *Civilized Shamans: Buddhism in Tibetan Societies*. Washington: Smithsonian Institution Press, 1993.

de Saussure, Ferdinand. "Course in General Linguistics" *Critical Theory Since 1965*. Edited by Hazard Adams and Leroy Searle. Gainesville: University Presses of Florida,1986. 646-654.

Schimmel, Annemarie. *Mystical Dimensions of Islam*. Chapel Hill: University of North Carolina Press, 1975.

Schlesier, Karl H. *The Wolves of Heaven: Cheyenne Shamanism, Ceremonies, and Prehistoric* . Norman: University of Oklahoma Press, 1987.

Schumacher, E. F. *Small is Beautiful: A Study Of Economics As If People Mattered*. London: Abacus, 1973.

Searle, John R. *The Rediscovery of the Mind*. London: The MIT Press, 1992.

_____. *The Construction of Social Reality*. New York: The Free Press, 1995.

_____. *Mind, Language, and Society*. New York: Basic Books, 1998.

Shah, Idries. *The Way of the Sufi*. London: Penguin Books, 1968.

Squires, Euan. *Conscious Mind in the Physical World*. Philadelphia: Institute of Physics Publishing, 1990.

_____. *The Mystery of the Quantum World*. Philadelphia: Institute of Physics Publishing, 1994.

Stapp, Henry P. *Mind, Matter, and Quantum Mechanics*. Springer-Verlag: New York, 1993.

_____. "Are Superluminal Connections Necessary", *Nuovo Cimento* 40B, 1977.

Stcherbatsky, Theodore. *The Conception of Buddhist Nirvāṇa*. New York: Gordon Press, 1973.

Sterba, James P. *Contemporary Social and Political Philosophy*. Belmont, California: Wadsworth Publishing Company, 1995.

_____. *Social and Political Philosophy: Classical Western Texts in Feminist and Multicultural Perspectives*. Belmont, California: Wadsworth Publishing Company, 1998.

Sutton, Florin Giripescu. *Existence and Enlightenment in the Lankavatara-sutra: A Study in the Ontology and Epistemology of the Yogacara School of Mahayana Buddhism*. Albany: State University of New York, 1991.

Suzuki, D. T. *The Lankavatara Sutra.* London: Routledge & Kegan Paul Ltd., 1966.

The Collected Works of Ramana Maharshi. ed. by Arthur Osborne. York Beach: Samuel Weiser, Inc., 1997.

The Encyclopedia of Philosophy, Vols. I-VIII. Edited by Paul Edwards. MacMillan Publishing Co., Inc.: New York, 1967.

The Tibetan Book of the Dead. translated by A. F. Thurman. New York: Bantam Books, 1994.

Tucci, Giuseppe. *On Some Aspects of the Doctrines of Maitreya[natha] and Asanga.* Calcutta: University of Calcutta, 1930.

Upaniṣads. translated by Patrick Olivelle. New York: Oxford University Press, 1996.

Ware, James R. *The Sayings of Mencius.* New York: Mentor Boks,1960.

Whitfill, Betsy. "Recovering the Soul: An Interview with Dr. Larry Dossey", *Share International.* Vol. 10, No. 7, (September 1991): 13-14.

Whitehead, Alfred North. *Process and Reality.* Corrected Edition. New York: The Free Press, 1978.

Whorf, Benjamin Lee. "The Relation of Habitual Thought and Behavior to Language" *Critical Theory Since 1965.* Edited by Hazard Adams and Leroy Searle. Gainesville: University Presses of Florida, 1986. 710-723.

Wollheim, Richard. *F. H. Bradley.* Penguin Books: Hammondsworth, Middlesex, 1959.

Zaehner, R. C. *Hindu and Muslim Mysticism.*
Rockport: Oneworld Publications, 1994.

Additional Readings in Esoteric Philosophy:

Bailey, Alice A. *The Ageless Wisdom Teachings (24 volumes).* Lucis Trust: New York, 1919-1949.

Blavatsky, Helena P. *The Secret Doctrine, Volume I, II & III.* Theosophical University Press: Pasadena, California, 1988.

_____. *Isis Unveiled, Volume I & II.* Theosophical University Press: Pasadena, California, 1998.

Jurriaanse, Aart. *Bridges.* 'Sun Centre' School of Esoteric Philosophy: Cape, South Africa, 1985.

Roerich, Helena. *The Agni Yoga Teachings (15 Volumes).* The Agni Yoga Society: New York, 1924-1939.

www.ingramcontent.com/pod-product-compliance
Lightning Source LLC
Chambersburg PA
CBHW060518100426
42743CB00009B/1368